SECRETS OF THE
PLAYSTATION2
AN UNAUTHORIZED GUIDE
TO THE HOTTEST ENTERTAINMENT MACHINE

INCLUDES
HINTS SECTION
AND A DIRECTORY OF
PS2 GAME
WEBSITES

AVAILABLE NOW

X-Men: Shadows of the Past
by Michael Jan Friedman

X-Men/Doctor Doom: The Chaos Engine, Book 1
by Steven A. Roman

Science of the X-Men
by Karen Haber and Link Yaco

Moebius' Arzach
by Randy and Jean-Marc Lofficier

Callisto Volume 1
by Lin Carter

West of Eden
by Harry Harrison

Mirage:
An Isaac Asimov Robot Mystery
by Mark W. Tiedemann

Arthur C. Clarke's Venus Prime Volumes 1, 2, and 3
by Paul Preuss

COMING SOON

X-Men/Magneto: The Chaos Engine, Book 2
by Steven A. Roman

Chimera:
An Isaac Asimov Robot Mystery
by Mark W. Tiedemann

Arthur C. Clarke's Venus Prime Volume 4
by Paul Preuss

Winter in Eden
by Harry Harrison

Share your thoughts about these and other ibooks titles
in the new ibooks virtual reading group at www.ibooksinc.com

SECRETS OF THE PLAYSTATION2

AN UNAUTHORIZED GUIDE
TO THE HOTTEST ENTERTAINMENT MACHINE

MICHELE E. DAVIS

ibooks

new york

www.ibooksinc.com

DISTRIBUTED BY SIMON & SCHUSTER, INC.

An Original Publication of ibooks, inc.

Distributed by Simon & Schuster, Inc.
1230 Avenue of the Americas, New York, NY 10020

Copyright © 2000 by ibooks, inc.

An ibooks, inc. Book

Distributed by Simon & Schuster, Inc.
1230 Avenue of the Americas, New York, NY 10020

ibooks, inc.
24 West 25th Street
New York, NY 10010

The ibooks World Wide Web Site Address is:
http://www.ibooksinc.com

You can visit the ibooks Web site for a free read and
download the first chapters of all the ibooks titles:
http://www.ibooksinc.com

ISBN 0-7434-1302-4
First ibooks, inc. printing October 2000
10 9 8 7 6 5 4 3 2
POCKET and colophon are registered trademarks of Simon & Schuster, Inc.

Edited by Steven Roman

Printed in the U.S.A.

TABLE OF CONTENTS

INTRODUCTION
A STAR (SYSTEM) IS BORN

Remember when the PlayStation2 was just an ethereal idea—a mass of hype and promise? The first glimpse critics had of the PS2 was through its protective glass box when it debuted at the 1999 Electronic Entertainment Expo (E3), the gaming industry's annual trade show in Los Angeles.

Reviewers said the new Sony machine was either going to be the next amazing revolution for games, or an unimpressive piece of hardware. Insiders insisted that, if Sega hadn't been able to gain market share until they built a product with a modem (the Dreamcast), how would Sony be able to pull off the biggest coup in gaming history?

Those of us who were gaming fanatics read every juicy detail we could get our hands on, questions pirouetting in our heads. What is it, really? What special features will be included? When will it be available?

Shortly after the system was shown for the first time, specs were revealed for public viewing, but they were vague, and labeled as "still in development." This left critics suspicious of the PS2 merits. But gleaming out of the specs were the shiny letters "DVD." It was revealed that the PlayStation2 would not only play DVD movies, but would feature Sony's non-interlaced DVD playback equipment, which would allow the screen to be refreshed all at once like a computer monitor.

Before feeling unaffected by this revelation, keep in mind that it implies you'll be able to plug a monitor into the new PlayStation.

So, the PlayStation2 was going to be a reality, and since most Sony fans already owned upwards of $1000 in PSX games, logically the question on every PS1 game owners lips was, "Will it be backward compatible?" Mum was the initial word from Sony, but the company then announced that the new machine would not only play most original PSX games, but would also offer better graphics and the technology to make many games load faster.

Once developers got their hands on the PS2, more reviews flooded online fanzines. Resounding through the development community was word that the PS2 was powerful, yet complicated—perhaps even a bit too complicated. When development houses started to dig into the depths of the PS2, they ended up over their heads. Conjecture reared its ugly head. Was the PlayStation2 too hard to program for?

Now, though, most developers are humming the PlayStation2 tune, citing innovation and technological savvy as the answers to the complicated, open technology on which the PS2 is built.

On March 6, 2000, Sony launched the PlayStation2 in Japan—a beta-test version allowing customers to sample the new equipment, thus giving the manufacturer time to work out potential system bugs before shipping the product to Europe and the U.S. With this strategy, Sony hoped to dodge potential problems like those encountered following the Dreamcast launch in Japan, a failure due mostly to weak marketing and a poor game lineup (at least in the opinion of gamers).

Weeks before the PS2 launch, there seemed to be a shortage of quality titles, with only *Tekken Tag Tournament* and *Ridge Racer V* having brand appeal. There were twelve other games, however, ranging from RPGs to racers to fighting games and strategies. The lineup was: *Eternal Ring* (adventure), *Kessen* (strategic simulation), *Popolocrois 3* (romantic animation), *Unison* (dance action and simulation), *DrumMania* (action), *Den-Sen Electric Lines* (action), *A-Train* (simulation), *Street Fighter EX3* (fighting), *Morita Shogi* (strategy), *Kakinoki Shogi* (strategy), *Doukyu Billiards 2* (simulation), and *Stepping Selection* (dancing arcade).

Even with this game turn-out it looked like the PS2 debut might go disastrously wrong, but Japan's loyalty to the Sony brand led to the sell-out of one million available units within days. Japanese gamers who snapped up the new PS2 bought DVDs to watch until new games hit the stores.

What's in store for Americans? Possibly a greater launch then the lucrative and incredibly successful Dreamcast debut of 1999. It is believed that there are currently at least 270 games in development for the North American version of the PlayStation2.

Because of the non-interlaced DVD viewing capability, the backward compatibility and the unusually complicated and expensive nature of the machine, people were estimating that the PS2, which sold for the equivalent of $370.00 in Japan, might retail for us much as $470.00 in the U.S. The feasibility of that price tag—given the game market of today—was ridiculous. Ears to the track and keen to the market, Sony wisely priced the unit at a tidy $299.99, the same price the first PSX was at its launch.

Quite the competitive price point, considering that it includes a DVD player, which normally retail for around $150.00-$200.00 themselves. But it's a strategy that seems to be working already. According to a January 2000 research report released by investment house Merrill Lynch, 100 million PS2 units are estimated to ship by Sony's fiscal year 2004 (ending in March of that year).

Now that Internet broadband still has focus, Sony stated that there will be no modem, but they are bringing out a network card that can be used on dial-ups. Is there a future for online gaming? Will people drop the cash for the chance to play *Ridge Racer* across the country? Only time will tell, but if you read the Usenet groups, lots of people want that challenge.

The competition for PS2 is tough. Sega. Nintendo. Microsoft. All the hubbub of the X-Box. The tug-of-war for market share is going to be fierce, and there are no sure winners at this point. Expect the battles to be fought with multimillion-dollar marketing campaigns that focus on lucrative licenses and exclusive titles.

It's going to be insanely exciting, if nothing else.

I.

JUST THE FACTS

As mentioned before, the PlayStation2 found a welcoming crowd of buyers in Japan, selling around two million units during the first four months of release. However, even the best-selling PS2 game has only sold 500,000 copies at the most, compared to Nintendo64 and PlayStation games which often sell well over a million copies.

When the original PSX launched in 1995, the average Japanese consumer was purchasing three games during the console purchase. Within the first two weeks of the PS2 launch, however, the ratio was less than one game per system sold.

In addition, within one month of the PS2's launch, DVD movie sales doubled in Japan. It's obvious that Sony has succeeded in making the PlayStation2 more than a simple video game console.

COMPETITION

Most manufacturers are vying for gaming system space in your living room, den, kid's room, or bedroom, and that includes Sony PlayStation, Sega Dreamcast, Nintendo64, and Microsoft's X-Box. Right now, though, the PS2 is the fastest machine out there.

MICROSOFT'S X-BOX

The X-Box specs are reminiscent of a PC. Microsoft's device contains a high-end AMD Athelon processor, a high-end NVidia GeForce video card, a DVD-ROM drive, a hard drive, a modem, and lots and lots of RAM. Rumors vary about whether the X-Box will have a Windows-based operating system.

Windows and DirectX on the X-Box will make it easier to port games from the PC to the new console, or to design them from scratch, since so many designers today are familiar with the DirectX APIs. Everything crammed into the X-Box indicates that it is poised to conquer the video game console market.

Bad news, though: Initially, there was going to be a head-to-head battle for market share between Microsoft and Sony around the holiday season, but now Microsoft claims to be eighteen months away from final product. The official word was that Microsoft had a choice: release a less sophisticated device for Christmas 2000, or a more sophisticated device for Christmas 2001. Microsoft chose the more sophisticated box.

SEGA DREAMCAST

After pushing hard to get Sega to adopt Windows CE as the operating system for the Dreamcast, nothing has been heard about Windows CE or its DirectX components since the gaming device's launch.

However, Sega has seen the way of the future: online gaming. On April 3, 2000, Sega announced that they would give away the Dreamcast to anyone who signed up for two years with their online gaming service, SegaNet. I suspect we will be seeing more such deals in the future from the other console developers.

NINTENDO

Nintendo64 is a reality, but Nintendo already has another gaming device in the works, internally named "Dolphin." They have been secretive about this project, but it does appear to be a next generation console, and DVD-based. The skinny is that it features an IBM Gekko Processor, which is an extension of the IBM Power PC Architecture, with a 400 MHz Clock Speed, and a semiconductor process 0.18 micron copper technology. By allying themselves with IBM, Nintendo should have no problem making enough systems to meet the demand, and they will probably have a reasonable price tag.

Item	PS2	PS1	N64	Dreamcast
Polygon Power	20m/sec	360,000/sec	150,000/sec	3m/sec
Main Clock Speed	300 MHz	33.86MHz	93.75MHz	200MHz
Memory	32MB	2MB	4MB	16MB
Mem Bus Bandwith	3.2GB/s	132MB/s	500MB/s	N/A

WHO IS GOING TO BUY A PS2

Given the differences, and the fact that the PlayStation2 is faster and can run more complicated games then its competition, it seems like only diehard gamers would be purchasing it, but that's not the case. This machine is not just for the diehard gamers, nor is it an Atari 2600, or Colecovision that could be obsolete in ten years.

The PS2 is a visionary machine because of what it can offer in the future. Right now you look at the specs and see lots of numbers that mean one thing: a better gaming machine. But the vision behind this "better gaming machine" are things like the ability to run a Web browser, and forays into more complicated online environments—not just gaming either, but also proprietary portals. And who knows what will show up on them . . . ?

If there is a hierarchy of important things about the PlayStation2 that would help you make up your mind because you aren't sold yet, here's a list:

* PlayStation2 games
* Backward compatibility
* DVD movie playback
* Gateway to broadband

If you're thinking, "Geez, broadband—that's going to be more money," fear not! Sony has already hinted that the wave of the future for broadband is a subscription plan where you would get the adapter because you're a subscriber.

2.
PLAYSTATION2 HARDWARE
(OR TECH-HEADS, START YOUR ENGINES)

PHYSICAL OVERVIEW

The PS2 weighs 4 lbs. 10 oz and measures 12" by 7" by 3". It uses Sony's 128-bit, 295 MHz "Emotion Engine" chip.

APPEARANCE

The PlayStation2 can sit vertically:

Or the PlayStation2 can sit horizontally:

What's Included and What's Optional

The PlayStation2 comes with some standard features. Sony, however, hopes that you will be shopping for enhancements to its system.

Controller ports

Surprisingly, there are only two controller ports on the system. Sony announced a multitap for PS2 which will enable four players to join in on one game. Also, expect online options to play a big part of Sony's future.

The Airplay Controller

Eleven Engineering delivered a new controller peripheral for the PlayStation this year, called Airplay. It isn't like any other controller, though—what makes it special is the fact that it has become one of the first radio communication (RC) controllers on the market.

In a general way, this allows you to utilize the controller and play games from virtually any direction—and any place—in the home. The RC feature is much more advanced than the simple (and usual) infrared feature, as it can operate at longer distances (up to 7 meters/25 feet), maintain batteries for longer periods of time, and utilize powerful and diverse radio channels that can't be blocked.

Up to sixteen Airplay controllers can be used within the same area, and a programmable feature allows for different buttons to have certain assigned purposes. The controller launched in the U.S. for $39.99

Eleven is currently developing the Airplay2, a controller

that will feature both wireless gaming and the added benefit of a built-in DVD remote control for the PS2.

MODEM

Sony has officially stated it will not ship the machine with a modem. However, the system will use a modem for several purposes. Sony will enable gamers to choose from USB, IEEE 1394 Firewire (identified as "i-Link" by Sony) and PCMCIA PC Card interfaces.

KEYBOARD

The PS2 has a USB port which will take a USB keyboard. This will be a likely addition if you're doing anything outside of game playing on your PS2. Sony has yet to release the keyboard, though.

HARD DISK DRIVE (HDD)

The US PS2 has a PC Card Type III slot on the back that will accept a hard drive. Sony has yet to release the HDD, though.

DVDs

DVD—which once stood for Digital Video Disc or Digital Versatile Disc—is the next generation of optical disc storage technology. DVD video resolution uses 500 horizontal lines, compared to 425 for a laserdisc and 240 for VHS. Besides the improvement over VHS for sound and picture quality, there is a slew of different features that DVDs provide.

INSTANT REWIND

Because DVDs are split into chapters that operate the same as tracks on a CD, you can skip between them and the movie will start from that point. There is no need for the movie to rewind or fast forward.

EXTRA FOOTAGE

Extra footage, cut scenes, alternate endings—anything that didn't make the final cut is usually included on the DVD version of movies.

DURABILITY

You know the more you play a VHS tape the more broken up the images become. With a DVD you can play the movie as many times as you want without losing any picture or sound quality.

CAMERA ANGLES

You have the option of storing up to nine different camera angles on a DVD. If the movie you're watching includes this feature you can switch views on the fly.

SUBTITLES

My Barbie-owning hairstylist was amazed that she could rent a foreign film on DVD and not have subtitles. Yup, you read that right. DVDs allow you to select between subtitles or dubbing. You even get to pick what language you want everything in: French, Spanish, English, your choice.

DVD has the capacity for up to eight separate audio tracks and thirty-two subtitle tracks. Often the extra audio tracks include a running commentary from the director or actors on the film, where they recount behind-the-scene reports and anecdotal information. The *Apocalypse Now* DVD, for example, has an especially cool director monologue.

WIDE-SCREEN FORMAT ALLOWED

Most DVD titles give you the option of viewing the movie in either wide-screen, "letterbox" format—which is what you see in movie theatres—or in full-screen, where the picture fits your entire TV screen, no matter what size it is.

EXTRAS

Included on the DVD are all kinds of bonus features, including cast biographies, trailers, storyboards, director or actor interviews, music videos, and mini-games.

THE PS2 MOTHERBOARD: SYSTEM SPECS

It looks like the PlayStation2 will be the most powerful console system for quite a while, at least until the Microsoft X-Box or Nintendo Dolphin are unveiled. With that in mind, here's the skinny on what makes the PlayStation2 the beast that it is.

CPU
* System Clock: 300MHz
* Co-Processor: FPU (Floating Point Multiply Accumulator x1, Floating Point Divider x1)
* Vector Units: VU0 & VU1(Floating Point Multiply Accumulator x9, Floating Point Divider x1)
* Floating Point Performance: 6.2 GFLOPS 3D CG Geometric Transformation: 66 million Polygons per second
* Compressed Image Decoder: MPEG2 Graphics

* Clock Frequency: 150MHz
* DRAM Bus bandwidth: 48 GB Per Second
* DRAM Bus width: 2560 bits
* Pixel Configuration: RGB: Alpha:Z Buffer (24:8:32)
* Maximum Polygon Rate: 75 Million Polygons Per Second Perspective-Correct Texture Mapping Point, Bilinear, Trilinear and Anisotropic Mip-map filtering Gouraud shading Z-buffer
* Colored Light Sourcing: 16.7 million colors
* Hardware based fog, bump mapping, and texture compression Shadow and light volumes
* Super sampling

MEMORY
* System Memory: 32 MB Direct Rambus
* Memory Bus Bandwidth: 3.2 GB per second

SOUND
* Number of voices: ADPCM: 48 channel on SPU2 plus definable by software
* Sampling Frequency: 44.1 KHz or 48 KHz (selectable)

INPUT
* Dedicated I/O Processor: PlayStation CPU+
* Clock Frequency: 33.8 MHz or 36.8MHz (selectable)

STORAGE MEDIA
* DVD-ROM (CD-ROM compatible)
* 4.8 Gigabyte data storage
* 24X CD-ROM, 4x DVD-ROM speed

PORTS/EXPANSION
* 2 standard PlayStation controller ports
* 2 standard PlayStation memory card slots
* 1 AV multicable output (Composite, S-Video, RGB?)
* 2 USB ports
* 1 optical digital output
* 1 Type III PCMCIA card slot
* 1 iLink port (IEEE1394/FireWire)

OTHER
* 8-Meg Memory Card

FAQs

How is original PlayStation compatibility maintained with all this new hardware?

Because the system's I/O (input/output) processor is essentially the core, or main processor, of the original PlayStation, the system will include this processor to insure backward compatibility with all existing PlayStation games. Sony will most likely continue to institute the territorial lockout to make sure that only U.S. PlayStation2s play original U.S. PlayStation games.

Will it use CDs or DVDs?

The PlayStation2 will have a DVD drive that is capable of reading both CD-formatted (650 megabytes) discs as well as DVD-formatted discs (4.7 gigabytes). Most of the initial games will be straight CD games; however, as time progresses, more and more games will be produced on DVD.

Sony announced that it has developed a specially designed spindle that can read both DVDs and CDs from the same laser. Normal DVD readers have two sets of lasers: one to read CDs, and one to read the finer pits of a DVD. This measure of combining the laser functionality will reduce the cost of the PlayStation2's manufacturing in the long run.

Can it play DVDs?

Sony has said that, right out of the box, the PlayStation2 will indeed have the ability to play DVD movies. Sony has official plans to release a hard drive-like peripheral in the year 2001 to coincide with its broader e-commerce scheme. This will enable players to buy games, or perhaps update games, as well as movies, and music online. The system has MPEG2 capabilities, too.

Since DVD is still rather new at the moment, only a minority of people have dedicated DVD players in their homes. My local video store guru, Kai, said that the holiday season would net lots of DVD players for people. For many, the PS2 will be the perfect solution, since for the price of a console, you basically get a free DVD player. It certainly won't be as full-featured and robust as a dedicated player, but will suit the needs of most users just fine.

How many polygons can it handle?

Since a 3D object is constructed of pieces (known as polygons), the number of polygons per second a system can process indicates how detailed the 3D graphics can be, and how smoothly they can animate.

Officially, the maximum number the system can

process is seventy-five million polygons per second. But this number doesn't take into account texture maps (images wrapped onto the polygon set), filtering (making the textures look clean, natural, and unpixelated), and lighting (giving the object a more 3D look with realistic shadows and light effects). With all this into place, the PlayStation2 can process twenty million polygons per second. Again, this number will be affected by in-game physics, character artificial intelligence, audio, and other processor-intensive effects. I'll take a conservative estimate and say initial games will push around eight to ten million polygons per second— and believe me when I say that this number is still no slouch.

What kind of effects can it do?

Obviously the system will be capable of mip-mapping, bi-linear filtering, anti-aliasing, texture-correction, and Z-buffering. Sony has also touted that the system will handle Bezier surfacing, a technique that decides how many polygons are needed to make an object have smoother surfacing. Bezier surfacing also assists in telling the object to use as many or as few polygons as the system can handle at that processing moment. Developers can easily insert Bezier-surfaced CG models into the PlayStation2 and the system will be able to render the object in real-time.

3.
NORTH AMERICA VS. JAPAN
THE PS2 DIFFERENCES

The North American PS2 was physically altered to enable Sony to plug a Hard Disc Drive (HDD) into the system's back end. This was done to enable players to eventually buy a separate HDD, for downloading movies, games, music, and other data. The PCMCIA card slot is now Type III. Type III is physically big enough to hold a small hard drive.

The PS2 did not ship in Japan with a hard drive, and that's going to cause problems in the long run for developers simply because all the machines sold worldwide will not be the same. Since Japan is the source for most kick-ass games, the lack of a hard drive will put that market at a disadvantage.

This new configuration doesn't require a card to play DVDs like the Japanese version. The North American version has DVD drivers built into the hardware itself, instead of using the software drivers placed on the Memory Cards. This will hopefully prevent copying from DVD to other media, and solves data corruption problems on the PS2 Memory Cards, too.

What peripheral hardware is available?

There are several companies, such as Mad Catz and Nyko, that are developing everything from remote controllers and steering wheels to memory cards for the PS2.

Mad Catz is producing two products: the Mad Catz Memory, Silver, Gold and Platinum high-capacity, uncompressed memory cards; and 900MHz Wireless Dual Force Controllers, the world's first analog RF controller for PlayStation which includes a built-in rechargeable Ni-cad battery with docking/recharge station. Check 'em out at out: http://www.madcatz.com/

Nyko (http://www.nyko.com/html/main.html) offers controllers, special controllers, memory cards, accessories, adapters, and cables. This is cool! The Scorpion is a dual analog controller with built-in dual shock, independent button for turbo and an LED slow motion indicator, and it comes in difference colors, just like an iMac.

NORTH AMERICAN PERIPHERALS

*PS2 Analog controller (DUAL SHOCK 2) [SCPH-10010] (U.S. $34)

*PS2 Memory Card (8MB) [SCPH-11020] - (U.S. $34)

*PS2 Mutitap (four slots for both controllers and memory cards) (U.S. $34)

*PS Hard Drive (HDD) (No official U.S. price yet)

Expect cables, stands, and more to be announced later.

JAPANESE PERIPHERALS

* Analog controller (DUAL SHOCK 2) [SCPH-10010] - (U.S. $32)

*PlayStation2 Memory Card (8MB) [SCPH-11020] - (U.S. $32)

* AV Cable (integrated audio/video) [SCPH-10030] - (U.S. $9)

*PlayStation2 Vertical Stand [SCPH-10040] - (U.S. $14)

*AC Power Code [SCPH-10050] - (U.S. $4)

*S-Video Cable [SCPH-10060] - (U.S. $28)

*RFU Adapter [SCPH-10070] - (U.S. $23)

* AV Adapter [SCPH-10080] - (U.S. $11)

*PlayStation2 Multitap [SCPH-10090] - (U.S. $33)

*PlayStation2 Component AV Cable - (U.S. $23)

*PlayStation2 Horizontal Stand [SCPH-10110] -(U.S. $9)

ANALOG DUAL SHOCK CONTROLLER

The Sony controller probably looks familiar, and that's because it's a modification of the PlayStation's highly successful Dual Shock pad. With built-in vibration functions, all analog buttons and twin analog sticks, the Dual Shock 2 is probably the most versatile controller.

However, since it's so similar to the original, you'll probably feel that the Dual Shock 2 has the same plusses and minuses as the original pad. So, count on a great ergonomic grip with a stiff D-Pad, and all analog buttons.

PERIPHERAL COMPATIBILITY

While the PlayStation2 will have its own specific controllers, memory cards and peripherals, all original PlayStation memory cards, controllers, even the PocketStation (see below) will work on the PlayStation2. This will insure 100% backward compatibility.

Will the current PlayStation be able to play new PlayStation2 games?

Unfortunately, no. PlayStation2 games will be written specifically for PS2 hardware, and the current PlayStation will not recognize the instructions on a PlayStation2 game disc.

HARDWARE THAT'S COMING SOON

AV Multi Cable [SCPH-10120]: Undecided

The standard PlayStation2 memory card has 8 MB of memory, and packs more storage than the old PlayStation 1 cards did. They're a lot faster by over 200 times, so no more waiting thirty seconds for your game to save in RPGs. The PlayStation2 comes with one card, but who knows exactly how long a single card will last you? Hopefully you won't need a slew of them around to save your basic scores.

One item that's been unofficially confirmed is a Headset and Voice-Recognition system, which Sony won't speak about yet.

POCKETSTATION

The PocketStation is a miniature game console onto which you can download specially designed games from your PlayStation via its Memory Card slot. Games for PocketStation are stored on the same disc as PlayStation games, and can enhance PlayStation games with added features—for example, by using PocketStation you may be able to train characters in your favorite PlayStation game while sitting on the bus. You can also download stand-alone PocketStation games.

You can swap game data between your Play and PocketStations, and it also allows multi-player gaming via the built-in Infared data link. As well as a pocket games console, PocketStation acts as a standard PlayStation memory card. Currently, the PocketStation is only available in Japan, and has sold over four million units!

What do the different colored discs mean?

There are three colored discs:
* Blue is for PS2 CD-ROM
* Silver is for PS2 DVD
* Black stands for the original PlayStation disc

MULTI-PLAYER GAMES

Sony has officially announced that a new PS2 multitap will ship at launch, which means at least four-player support. No currently announced games have multi-player capabilities for more than four players, although Sony will announce a more comprehensive online strategy later on in 2000, and may announce multi-player online gaming then.

Of course, the most powerful system in the world would be nothing if there were no games developed for it, so it's good to know that the PlayStation2 will have them in spades. The rock-solid developer support of the original PlayStation has carried over to the PS2, and we all know how many games the PlayStation has; PS2 owners will have plenty of quality titles to enjoy. With key third parties such as Konami, Capcom, Namco, and Square, there's no question that the PS2 will be swimming in quality games.

What about online games?

How about:
* *Star Trek Conquest Online*
* *Final Fantasy X*
* *Final Fantasy XI*
* *Gekikuukan Pro Baseball*
* *Driving Emotion Type-S* (Square)

EXTRAS

Fear not, memory card lovers, for you can buy these wondrous pieces of plastic for $34.00 a piece. Also retailing alongside the machine will be more controllers and multitaps to plug those controllers into—all for $34.00 each. The games will set you back $49.00 per title—about as much as a debuting PSX title, but like anything else, hopefully prices will drop after several months . . . or you could buy original PlayStation games to sate your appetite.

4.
RATING GAMES
HOW IT WORKS, AND HOW IT APPLIES

Even though the Japanese market seemed slim on games when the PS2 made its debut, the United States and European markets look pretty good in terms of immediate PlayStation2 offerings, and games that arrive on the scene shortly thereafter.

Some games are being ported over to the PlayStation2 originally having been a Nintendo, PC, or Sega game, and others are made especially for Sony or by Sony. Most of them take advantage of the amazing new system, its fast load times, incredible graphic, and overall quality.

But before you go to your local gaming outlet in search of what promise to be the coolest games around, there's one very important thing you need to be familiar with—a short alphabet of sorts that determines exactly for which age groups a game can be aimed.

Welcome, friends and fans, to the Entertainment Software Ratings Board rating system for games.

Because a lot of games we'll be showing you in the next chapter are in approval, or haven't been rated yet, it's best to know how to look for these ratings, and what they mean, before you go to the store.

Look for these ratings on the front of the package and, for more information, look for content descriptors on the back of the package.

EARLY CHILDHOOD

Titles rated "Early Childhood (EC)" have content suitable for children ages three and older and do not contain any material that parents would find inappropriate.

KIDS TO ADULTS

Titles rated "Kids to Adult (K-A)" have content suitable for persons ages six and older. These titles will appeal to people of many ages and tastes. They may contain minimal violence, some comic mischief or some crude language.

EVERYONE

In 1998, the new "Everyone" designation replaced the "Kids to Adults" rating, but the age range and content guidelines remain the same.

TEEN

Titles rated "Teen (T)" have content suitable for persons ages thirteen and older. Titles in this category may contain violent content, mild or strong language, and/or suggestive themes.

MATURE

Titles rated "Mature (M)" have content suitable for persons ages seventeen and older. These products may include more intense violence or language than products in the Teen category. In addition, these titles may also include mature sexual themes.

ADULTS ONLY

Titles rated "Adults Only (AO)" have content suitable only for adults. These products may include graphic depictions of sex and/or violence. "Adults Only" products are not intended to be sold or rented to persons under the age of eighteen.

RATING PENDING

Product has been submitted to the ESRB and is awaiting final rating.

CONTENT DESCRIPTORS

When you look on the back of a package, you may see any of the following phrases that further describe the product's content:

VIOLENCE

Mild Animated Violence: Contains scenes involving animated or pixelated characters in the depiction of unsafe or hazardous acts or violent situations.

Mild Realistic Violence: Contains scenes involving characters in the depiction of unsafe or hazardous acts or violent situations in realistic or photographic detail.

Comic Mischief: Scenes depicting activities that have been characterized as slapstick or gross vulgar humor.

Animated Violence: Contains depictions of aggressive conflict involving animated and pixilated characters.

Realistic Violence: Contains realistic or photographic-like depictions of body parts.

Animated Blood and Gore: Animated/pixilated or cartoon-like depictions of mutilation or dismemberment of body parts.

Realistic Blood and Gore: Representations of blood and/or gore in realistic or photographic-like detail.

Animated Blood: Animated/pixilated or cartoon-like depictions of blood.

Realistic Blood: Representations of blood in a realistic or photographic-like detail.

LANGUAGE

Mild Language: Product contains the use of words like "damn."

Strong Language: Commonly referenced four-letter words, including anatomical references.

SEXUAL CONTENT

Suggestive Themes: Mild provocative references or material.

Mature Sexual Themes: Contains provocative material: including depiction of the human body either animated or photographic-like formats.

Strong Sexual Content: Graphic depiction of sexual behavior and/or the human form (i.e., frontal nudity) in either animated or photographic-like detail.

At the time of this book's printing, most games either haven't started their ESRB rating review period, or the games that have already been submitted to the ESRB are waiting for final ratings.

5.
THE GAMES
(IN OTHER WORDS, THE GOOD STUFF)

PLEASE NOTE: If a game in this chapter isn't mentioned in detail, it's because there wasn't any news available at the time this book went to press. For the time being, many developers are keeping screenshots and other product information under tight control.

ACTION

At this time, there are plenty of action games to choose from—a total of thirty games so far, with the promise of many more yet to come.

Aliens: Colonial Marines
Armored Core 2
Army Men: Air Attack 2
Army Men: Sarge's Heroes 2
Bomberman 2001
D-Jump!
Den-sen
Dragon's Lair 3D
Gradius III & IV: Myth of Resurrection
Gungriffon Blaze
Maximo
The Mechsmith Run
Medal of Honor PS2
Mobile Suit Gundam
Navy SEALs
No One Lives Forever
Oni
Panic Surfing

*Rayman 2: The Great Escape
*Red Faction
*Robocop
*Silpheed: The Lost Planet
*Soul Surfing
*Splash Dive
*Spy Hunter
*Star Wars: Starfighter
*Timesplitters
*Top Gun
*Unreal Tournament
*The World is Not Enough
*X Squad

ALIENS: COLONIAL MARINES

Fox Interactive (www.foxinteractive.com) and Check-Six Games bring you *Aliens: Colonial Marines*. Based on the popular *Aliens* film series, this game delves into the background of the United States Colonial Marine Corps (USCMC), explaining the Corps' history, squad tactics, and weapons.

It's squad-based, not single-shooter, so you have extra help in dealing with the droves of Aliens that are bearing down on you, double-sets of teeth gnashing. The cool thing is that you'll get realistic animation and 3D-modeling.

You may not have heard of Check-Six, probably because they didn't have any games under their belt before this one. However, the development team consists of people who worked on previous hi-tech-based titles like *Mechwarrior 2* and *Heavy Gear 2*, and the *Starship Troopers: Roughnecks* CG cartoon series.

ARMORED CORE 2

From Software comes the mech-simulation/action game *Armored Core 2* for the PS2, with a similar premise to that of *Battletech*: It is the distant future, and a catastrophic war has wiped out most of mankind. Giant corporations have come to the forefront to battle for control of the remnants of civilization and their weapons of choice are giant war machines (ACs).

You take the role of a mercenary who receives money for completing various missions for the different corporations. This money is put towards purchasing numerous AC upgrades necessary to complete the more difficult missions.

There is an incredible amount of customization you can make to your AC, including modifying parts and weapons for your robot. For example, you can choose from four different styles of legs: humanoid legs, reverse jointed legs, caterpillar treads, and four-leg hovers.

Armored Core 2

BOMBERMAN 2001

Bomberman 2001 by Hudson Soft is a multi-player game that has been available for other platforms; you can, however, play in one-player mode, where you run around and blow up stuff with three types of bombs: fire, earth, and water.

In multi-player mode you can have a split screen where each player races to the end of a level. Another mode is called, "Story," where enemies have energy meters and you can design different endings.

D-JUMP!

Ubi-Soft's *D-Jump!* lets you play a Rastafarian lead character, and players engage in a time-traveling adventure to find out why he is slowly turning into wood.

Twenty enlightening worlds are available for non-stop action and adventure.

DEN-SEN

SCEI, in conjunction with Sony, is creating *Den-Sen*, which is the Japanese name for the electric wires around a city that guide and power buses and trains. In third-person point of view, you control a female character riding around on those wires using a coat hanger.

Amazingly, it pretty much plays like a roller coaster, and you have to jump her from one line to another or she drops to her death.

GRADIUS: MYTH OF RESURRECTION

Konami (www.konami.com) is introducing the sixteen-shooter game *Gradius*, with two games, *Gradius III* and *Gradius IV*, bundled on the same disc. It's basically a direct port of the two side-scrolling space arcade games with minor enhancements.

Trademark *Gradius* weapons and defensive items are included, such as the twin forward shields, and the triple drone orbs that duplicate the movements of your ship. Power-ups have been graphically enhanced and the audio upgraded to take advantage of the PS2.

Comparing *Gradius III* and *IV*, *IV* allows you to select six different power-up paths at the start of the game and then set out to defeat your enemies. Unique bosses and enemies such as giant Easter Island-style stone heads and scary mechanized spiders make for a continuous challenge.

Some cool improvements are the environmental mapping and polygon morphing. Beginners will have an easier time with the easy play mode, and a stage selection and "continue" feature allows you to pick up wherever you left off, sort of like a DVD movie.

For more information, be sure to check out www.pc manager.com/planetgradius/PlanetGradius/planetgradius.html.

GUNGRIFFON BLAZE (GGB)

Capcom (www.capcom.com) and GameArts are developing a match for *Armored Core 2*. *GGB* is the sequel to the two Sega Saturn games *Gungriffon* and *Gungriffon II*.

Continuing the tradition of mech-based combat, this first-person action-shooter puts you in the cockpit, featuring multiple fighting machines called AWGS (Armored Walking Gun System) from countries around the future Earth; they include lightweight Japanese High-Macs 3, the Italian reconnaissance mech Valiant, the highly maneuverable German Sturm Hunter, and the French surface-to-air defense mech Super Autruche.

In the PS2 version, there is a new feature that enables you to attach optional equipment to customize your machine. Adding to the sensory detail are gun smoke, explosions, drifting clouds, and blowing sand drifts.

MEDAL OF HONOR PS2 (WORKING TITLE)

Ever since the release of the Steven Spielberg/Tom Hanks

film *Saving Private Ryan*, World War II has been a hot topic for producers both in Hollywood and the gaming industry (e.g., the *Army Men* series for PlayStation). Having proven that battling Nazis can be successfully translated to the gaming industry through the release of *Medal of Honor*—and its recent sequel, *MoH: Underground*—DreamWorks Interactive is in the midst of developing a version for the PlayStation2.

In the first-person shooter—which actually takes place between the third and fourth levels of the original *MoH*—your mission is to locate a secret German superweapon that could change the course of the war. Accompanying you will be three CPU-controlled allies: a demolitions expert, a medic/sniper (talk about a conflict of interests!), and a paratrooper/sergeant. In order to successfully complete the game, all four of "you" must survive; if anyone dies, the game ends.

Medal of Honor PS2 is scheduled for release in fall 2001.

MOBILE SUIT GUNDAM

Bandai (www.bandai.com/gd), who successfully brought *Gundam Wing* to the states, is bringing a new mech-animation game to PlayStation2. The premise is that you control a towering mech in the heat of battle, using both guns and blades to destroy your opponents.

Other *Gundam* games have featured one-on-one mech battles, but this version allows you to face multiple opponents for the first time. The power of the PlayStation2 allows the characters from the animé to be rendered in real-time, using polygons to accurately recreate their images.

NAVY SEALS

Navy SEALs is a tactical first-person shooter game that focuses on the special military tactics used by SEALs teams. For more information about what types of military tactics they use, take a look at: www.the-south.com/TheTeams and www.navyseals.com.

NO ONE LIVES FOREVER

Move over, Lara Croft—here's a female superspy who's part James Bond, part Austin Powers, and she's got even *bigger* guns! Set in the swingin' 1960s, this first-person shooter stars Agent Archer, a beautiful (of course) and deadly secret agent, with a whole carload of bad guys out to keep her from completing her mission.

Originally developed and released for the PC by Fox Interactive, look for *No One Lives Forever* to cross over to the PS2 sometime in 2001.

No One Lives Forever

ONI

Gamers were hoping that *The Matrix* would somehow end up as a game for PlayStation2, and it seems some of the action has, along with influences from animé classics like *Akira* and *Ghost in the Shell.*

This action adventure game stars Konoko, an elite agent of the Tech Crimes Task Force (TCTF). As Konoko, your mission is to bring down a ruthless crime syndicate in the hi-tech future of 2032. The gameplay, which the developers refer to as "full-contact action," is a mix of hand-to-hand combat and gunplay.

The cool thing is that when a punch is administered after a kick, you won't have to wait for the kick animation to end—it'll just seamlessly segue into the next move without the kind of animation "popping" that's present in some other games.

Rockstar Games (www.rockstargames.com/games/games.html) and Bungie Software (http://oni.bungie.com) are using AutoCAD pro's for authenticity and aesthetic detail.

Oni

RAYMAN 2: THE GREAT ESCAPE

Rayman, developed by Ubi-Soft (www.ubisoft.com/usa/rayman2), started out as a two-dimensional platformer, and then moved into 3D. The story is that robo-pirates from deep space capture and enslave the residents of a plant and only Rayman—an armless, legless, neckless hero who moves with athletic grace—escapes. He then has to save the world, and free his friends.

Rayman 2: The Great Escape

Rayman's planet is a lovingly envisioned place—it's almost like a Disney movie, with waterfalls tumbling into picture perfect blue pools while purple mushrooms bob gently in the breeze and butterflies whirl about Rayman.

RED FACTION

Red Faction (www.redfaction.com), by THQ and Volition, will change the way first-person shooting games are played.

The cool thing is the use of Geo-mad technology.

Geo-mad is real-time, arbitrary geometry modification that drastically enhances realism and diversity of game play. This means that, in the world of *Red Faction*, you are no longer bound by the walls around you. If you need to join the action on the other side of a brick wall, you can go there. No building is impenetrable, no tower is stable, and no haven is safe. With this real-time dynamic environment, *Red Faction* is a strategist's heaven.

SILPHEED: THE LOST PLANET

Developed by *Resident Evil* and *Dino Crisis* gaming company Capcom (www.capcom.com), *Silpheed: The Lost Planet* is a follow-up game to the original *Silpheed*, an action, overhead shooting game that was released for the Sega system. The premise is that you are the last hope for the survival of good in the universe, and you pilot a Silpheed starfighter in a race against time to defeat the evil computer that is threatening to destroy your people.

SPY HUNTER

Spy Hunter is one of the original driving/shooting arcade classics created by Midway Home Entertainment. Now we're talking! Atari2600 and ColecoVision were the first platforms to sport this game.

This classic puts you behind the wheel of a car that would make even 007 jealous. Being a spy isn't all fun and games though—bad guys are on the road and they want to see you dead. You can bump them off the road, blast 'em with your front grill machine guns, smoke 'em out with your smoke screen, or send 'em spinning through an oil slick of your design.

Sounds like a great Bond film, but where are the chicks?

STAR WARS: STARFIGHTER

LucasArts (www.lucasarts.com/products/starfighter) offers spectacular flight battles inspired by its *Star Wars* flight-game heritage.

The intensity of classic air and space combat games is combined in the fast-paced flight action game. Here you will be thrust into a series of dramatic missions by being in the shoes of one of three pilots that help save the planet Naboo from the powerful and menacing Trade Federation. As the story unfolds, you'll go through a series of dogfight-oriented missions that'll take place on planets and off in space.

TIMESPLITTERS

Eidos Interactive (www.eidosinteractive.com) has a couple of projects in the works, including *TimeSplitters*. Eidos and Free Radical Design have teamed up to develop this title.

As the player you will maneuver unique characters in the years between 1935 and 2035. You play in a somewhat first-person shooter genre that has the intensity of *Doom*, yet the gameplay is easier then *Unreal Tournament*.

As you begin, a bunch of human heroes and villains find that they share a common foe in the main characters. The main bad guy tries to manipulate the fate of humanity using shards of crystal to sow fear, greed and conflict throughout history.

There are numerous different action styles including "Death Match," "Capture the Bag," and "Last Stand" scenarios.

The cool thing is that you can play with 1-4 players—cooperative and competitive—or a split-screen battle, which makes the whole battle more fun!

UNREAL TOURNAMENT

From InfoGames comes *Unreal Tournament* (www.unreal tournament.com), a first-person multi-player shoot 'em up game along the likes of *Duke Nuke 'Em.*

Unreal Tournament pits player against player or player against computer in several modes, which include a king of the hill style mode called "Domination," and "Capture the Flag."

The iLink port (Firewire) is utilized in this game to allow PS2 systems to connect to each other and support four simultaneous players.

Unreal Tournament

THE WORLD IS NOT ENOUGH

Pierce Brosnan as James Bond comes to Sony PlayStation, courtesy of Electronic Arts (www.ea.com). It wouldn't be Bond without the exotic locations: Itanbul, and Baku. (The capital of Azerbaijan, Baku is located on the western shore of the Caspian Sea and is one of Azerbaijan's largest cities.)

And weapons—it wouldn't be Bond without some innovative means of destruction up his sleeve, like the teeny PK99 for a little assault rifle action.

Electronic Arts plans to make the environments totally interactive, so blowing away a wall with your rocket launcher won't seem like such a bad idea. The developers are also planning to keep the levels and situations open-ended, with multiple ways of beating a level or getting out of a trap.

X SQUAD

In production, *X Squad* was originally called *X-Fire* (pronounced "crossfire"). Electronic Arts offers up corridor-shooting action with teammates.

In the year 2037, a terrorist organization has kidnapped government scientists, and you conduct a military operation to free them. Just jumping into a room, guns blasting, won't always work, though. You'll have to rely on your squad's advanced AI to carry out your basic "shoot, defend, protect" orders.

ADVENTURE

Wanna live vicariously? Try an adventure or horror game for a new perspective on reality, or a thrilling ride behind someone else's eyes.

*Blair Witch Volume 1: Rustin Parr
*Carrier 2
*Clive Barker's Undying
*Dark Corners of the Earth
*Extermination
*Fantasy
*Flesh and Wire
*Flower Sun and Rain
*Gunslinger
*Legacy of Kain: Soul Reaver II
*MDK Armageddon
*Metal Gear Solid 2: Sons of Liberty
*Ninja Gaiden: Kunai
*O Story
*Oddworld: Munch's Oddysee
*Onimusha: Warlords
*Outcast 2

*Picassio
*Project Eden
*Run Like Hell
*Saffire
*Scandal
*Shadow of Destiny
*Silent Hill 2
*Titanium Angels
*Tomb Raider VI
*Virtual Ocean
*Warriors of Might and Magic
*Zone of the Enders

BLAIR WITCH VOLUME I: RUSTIN PARR

Don't go into the woods! Anyone who's seen the sleeper hit film of 1999 (and can't get the last thirty seconds out of their minds) know the kind of dangers that can be found in the woods outside Burkittsville, Maryland. It's there that you'll find the infamous Blair Witch—and she doesn't like visitors.

Spinning off from the concepts introduced in the fictitious documentary (yes, it was all made up!), this game—developed by Terminal Reality and released for the PC by Gathering of Developers—takes place in the 1940s, and explores one facet of the increasingly chilling Blair Witch mythos. The day after convicted child killer Rustin Parr is put to death for his crimes, supernatural investigator Doc Holliday shows up in Burkittsville to investigate Parr's claims that ghosts forced him to kill seven children. Unfortunately for ol' Doc, he's about to find more proof than he could ever want—in spades.

And, hey—who knew all those stick-men hanging from the trees could actually come to life . . . ?

CARRIER 2

Jaleco's *Carrier 2* is a nice survival horror game that may ascend to B-movie greatness. Action takes place on an aircraft carrier, against a nasty creature. Dynamic special agents will be shooting zombies and opening locked doors in this sequel.

CLIVE BARKER'S UNDYING

Thought the *Resident Evil* series was creepy? Did *Silent Hill* make you look over your shoulder every time you

Clive Barker's Undying

walked down a darkened street? Well, you ain't seen nothing yet. From Electronic Arts and the darkest corners of the mind of master horror writer Clive Barker—the man who gave us the cult classic films *Hellraiser* and *Nightbreed*—comes *Undying*, a first-person shooter.

Developed by DreamWorks Interactive, the game takes place in 1920s Ireland. Your character, Magnus, is contacted by an old friend named Jeremiah, who asks you to come to his estate to help him with a seriously deadly problem: His family is suffering under a strange curse, and four of his siblings have recently died. How strange is the curse? Well, the siblings have come back to (undead) life, and are trying to kill him.

So, where's the Stephen King game?

DARK CORNERS OF THE EARTH

Headfirst Productions is bringing horror writer H. P. Lovecraft's greatest piece of short fiction, "The Call of

Cthulhu," to PS2 with *Dark Corners of the Earth*. It should be a first-person perspective, a 3D horror adventure.

Dark Corners is based on a series of short stories that have come to be labeled the "Cthulu Mythos"—tales involving horrible, inhuman deities from the depths of the earth and the coldest reaches of space whose interference in human affairs drive people mad and create destruction on the earth. *Dark Corners* promises to be a role-playing game packed with suspense, horror, madness, and things mankind was never meant to know.

EXTERMINATION

Sony and DEEPSPACE Software bring this horror survival game, which was originally called *Panic Action* by its creators. It's another third-person, 3D shooter with *Resident Evil* influences. As a member of the American Special Forces Unit (ASFU), you must prohibit out-of-control entities created in a secret lab hidden somewhere in the South Pole from destroying the world.

FANTASY

Jelco is presenting another adventure/action-type game in the vein of *Gauntlet Legends*. Utilizing PlayStation2's multi-tap, this will be a multi-player game that is not currently online. *Fantasy* is planned to be a pentailogy, with this title the first in the series of five.

There will be over 100 different mythological scenarios from around the world, including Europe, Asia, and Central America. You will be able to create a character, and, like in *Dungeons & Dragons*, be able to grow the character and increase attributes that can be carried over to the next adventure and the proceeding discs.

FLESH AND WIRE

Running with Scissors (ouch!) presents *Flesh and Wire* (www.fleshandwire.com), where you take on the role of a negative attitude cop named Angus, who wakes up one day to find that a large biological organism called the Nullid has swallowed his town and that he himself is in the process of being swallowed up by a large glutinous mass. (Can you say the 1950s and *The Blob*?)

Angus discovers that he can control the "blob" with his mind, then takes it upon himself to rid his town (and the world) of the Nullid. At this point, Angus has been partially devoured, but is still functional as a hero.

GUNSLINGER

Scheduled for a spring 2001 release, *Gunslinger* is a third-person adventure set in the Old West, offering a branching storyline that allows the player to become either a hero or a villain. Although it'll help to work on the skills like two-handed shooting, horseback riding, and gambling (!), the game wouldn't live up to its title if, every now and then, it didn't require you to stand in the middle of a street at high noon, facing off against some tough hombre. Now, draw! Developed by Surreal, the creators of *Drakan*.

LEGACY OF KAIN: SOUL REAVER II

Another title for PS2 from Eidos (www.eidosinteractive.com) is *Legacy of Kain: Soul Reaver II*, a sequel to the acclaimed

Legacy of Kain: Soul Reaver.

You resume the role of Raziel and travel through time into Nosgoth's past to pursue Kain. In this game you encounter new enemies as you unearth the mysteries of Nosgoths' ancient races, and expose the schemes behind the corruption of the Pillars, and the vampire genocide.

You can shift between real-time and spectral or material realms, plus the game is interconnected, so there are no load times. Amazing! On top of that, the enemies you encounter are creepy human vampire-hunters, Sarafan warrior-priests, the undead, and multi-dimensional demons.

O STORY (LOVE STORY)

O Story is a movie adventure game release by Enix (www.enix.com), about a young man who dies in an accident but comes back in human form with spiritual help to find that ethereal of all things: the love of his life. However, if time runs out before he can find his true love, he disappears forever! As the ghost, you communicate with a young girl to warn her about upcoming trouble.

This game is a live-actors actioner, choose-your-own-adventure kind of game, where, as the story unfolds, you get to choose your next move from a list of actions you can take at that juncture. It takes two DVDs to package because of the different plotlines, and includes CG graphics and movie sequences.

MDK ARMAGEDDON

MDK2 is a buoyant game that places you in a bio-suit as an adventurous janitor on a mission to kill invading aliens.

At this time, Interplay (www.interplay.com/mdk/index.html) is keeping details about *MDK Armageddon* pretty quiet, but no doubt it will be a sequel to the Dreamcast's MDK2.

If it matches the other *MDK* titles you'll be hopping, floating, jumping, and shooting as you waste enemies with extreme prejudice. The developers' sense of humor seems to have carried over to this sequel, with the inclusion of a six-legged dog, and the hero, Kurt, who also has six legs.

METAL GEAR SOLID 2: SONS OF LIBERTY

Konami's sequel to the popular *Metal Gear Solid* brings even more tactical espionage and intrigue to the MGS universe.

Metal Gear Solid 2: Sons of Liberty

After secret plans for Metal Gear Rex have been leaked, organizations throughout the world now have access to Metal Gear Technology. You're wondering what the new project is? Metal Gear Ray.

Original gameplay exists, as well as a few extra moves, as well as added variety and unpredictability to enemy AI. The other cool detail is that Konami is trying to replicate elements like heat, moisture, and feeling the air around the player. How can the developers do it? Well, we'll have to wait and see.

NINJA GAIDEN: KUNAI

Team Ninja (of *Dead or Alive*) is developing the latest in the *Ninja Gaiden* series, which is being released by Temco. The previous games were: *Ninja Gaiden* (of course), *Ninja Gaiden II: The Dark Sword of Chaos*, and *Ninja Gaiden III: The Ancient Ship of Doom*.

The original game's premise is that you, as the protagonist Ryu Hayabusa, must make your way through four action-packed levels fighting against the dark empire. Armed with his katana and jumping and climbing skills, Ryu must battle levels filled with enemies.

ODDWORLD: MUNCH'S ODDYSEE

Oddworld Inhabitants and Infogrames' latest game, *Munch's Oddysee*, is a 3D cornucopia filled with real-time issues, like changing times of the day, and revolving seasons of the year.

Munch is the last remaining Gabbit, but he's also a Glukkon test subject, and Gabbit eggs are a rare Glukkon delicacy. Abe, the title character from the previous *Oddworld* games, returns to give Munch a hand in his adventures. They are both trying to restore life to their decimated land. Abe and Munch have different skills: Abe can possess living creatures, while Munch is able to control machines.

Oddworld: Munch's Oddysee

For more information, check out the official Web site: www.oddworld.com

ONIMUSHA: WARLORDS

Warlords, Capcom and Flagship's latest "survival horror" title in the Onimusha series, possesses the kind of nail-biting action you'll find in games like *Resident Evil* and *Dino Crisis*. Unlike those titles, however, this one takes place in medieval times. You're an ancient warrior who must rescue a kidnapped princess from the evil general Nobanaga's castle.

Not only do you fight with knives, blades, and swords, but you also solve puzzles. No pre-rendered backgrounds exist in *Onimusha*, only real-time polygonal environments, and polygonal characters, although you will still be confined to the same gameplay path, as in the *Resident Evil* games.

For more information, check out the official Web site:
www.capcom.co.jp/newproducts/consumer/onimusha/
index.html

PICASSIO

Fancy yourself a stealthy art thief, like Pierce Brosnan in
The Thomas Crown Affair? Well, here's your chance to be
one. *Picassio*—not to be confused with master painter
Pablo Picasso—comes from Promethean Designs
(www.prodesigns.com/picassio.htm). It allows you to pilfer
any number of different museum showcase items. The
catch is you can't kill anyone (although you can whack
guards on the head), and you can't get caught!

Picassio

And, just like Bond, or Brosnan, you get to muck
around with some cool apparatuses.

PROJECT EDEN

Project Eden takes place in a land where people lead dehumanized and often fearful lives because the planet has become extremely overpopulated with scum, yuppies, and some very unfriendly beasts in the future. Eidos (www.eidos interactive.com) and Core Designs have created a creepy place where mammoth sky towers house the wealthy, and the great unwashed swarm (the rest of humanity) at the bottom.

As the game unravels you can select first- or third-person views, and control four characters, all members of the Urban Protection Agency (read: cops). Switching between the four characters allows you to achieve different tasks, and you can remotely control robots and machinery.

Game enhancements are at a premium, with mirrored surfaces, bump mapping, environmental bump mapping, gloss mapping, and light mapping.

RUN LIKE HELL

Remember 1979's classic science fiction/horror flick *Alien*? In it, a mining ship, investigating an SOS, lands on a distant planet. The crew discovers some strange creatures and investigates. Most of them don't live long enough to regret it. The tagline for the movie was "In space, no one can hear you scream."

That tagline accurately describes Interplay and Digital Mayhem's new game *Run Like Hell*, and if I were you I would start now, since your odds for survival are minimal.

For more information, check out the official Web site: www.interplay.com/runlikehell/index2.html

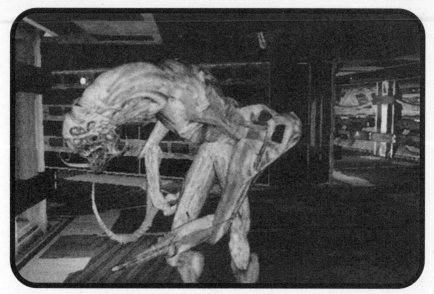

Run Like Hell

SHADOW OF DESTINY

A murder mystery with a twist is Konami's presentation in *Shadow of Destiny*. You play the murder victim(!), Eike Kusch. In the beginning of the story, you are murdered, but then gain the ability to time travel in order to prevent your own murder.

SILENT HILL 2

Konami's sequel to the original PSX game *Silent Hill* has been surrounded by rumors. However, during this year's E3, Sony plugged a demo of a scene found in the first game, now shown in real-time using the power of the PlayStation2's hardware.

   Silent Hill, released in 1999, introduced us to Harry Mason—a thirty-two-year-old writer whose wife just died—and his seven-year-old daughter, Cheryl. After a traffic accident on a road outside Silent Hill, Illinois, Harry and Cheryl become separated, and Harry is forced to search the darkened buildings and fog-shrouded streets of the town to locate his daughter. Standing in his way, however, are a legion of creatures let loose from the darkest nightmares. The game's true intent was to frighten us, something which very few games have been able to do. *Silent Hill* was successful in this endeavor because the game atmosphere was spooky, and unsettling. Just imagine what PS2 technology will do for the creep-factor in the sequel . . .

Brrrr.

For details and more screen shots go to: www.silenthill.com, or www.konami.com

TITANIUM ANGELS

A third-person action/adventure title by Sci (www.sci.co.uk), the creators of *Carmageddon*, *Titanium Angels* is set in an alternate future Earth with main characters Carmen Blake, bounty hunter, and Titan, a robot. The game takes advantage of Sci's proprietary 3D engine which makes possible a number of features, including curved surfaces, bump-mapping, and volumetric fogging and shadows.

What this means for you is that the game will have a natural feel to it, with cool special effects, and rendering will be less blocky on the screen.

TOMB RAIDER VI

Actually, it seems that won't be the title of the game when it's released in spring 2001. According to recent rumors, TR developer Core Design may be changing the series title of

Lara Croft's adventures to reflect the fact the her days of tomb raiding are now behind her. (Although it's more than likely that the upcoming summer 2001 movie starring Academy Award-winning actress Angelina Jolie will retain the *Tomb Raider* name, if only for recognition purposes).

Whatever the final title might be, you can expect more of the kind of two-fisted action, globe-hopping, and puzzle-solving that made Lara the PlayStation's premiere game girl.

ZONE OF THE ENDERS

A 3D mech action game from Konami, the folks who brought you *Metal Gear Solid*. The gameplay seems reminiscent of Sega's *Virtual On* series, which features huge mechs battling it out, with several ways to defeat each other.

Enders' adventure elements are similar to the roaming aspects of *The Legend of Zelda*, where the protagonist, Link, travels through an overhead game world populated with caves, hidden passages, oceans and enemies. He also has to explore room-based dungeons and use keys or bombs to open up doors to new rooms.

Exploration and interaction with environments and characters are heavily emphasized in *Zone of the Enders*. Action is held together by anime-style 3D cut scenes.

The story revolves around Orbital Frames, a key twenty-second century war machine used in interplanetary warfare. As young protagonist Leo Stenbuck, you seek vengeance upon Z.O.E., the Martian militia group that laid waste to your home colony.

Zone of the Enders

ARCADE

Arcade games range from the standard retro fare like *Pong* or *Space Invaders* to the county fair shooting range practice.

American Arcade
Gauntlet: Dark Legacy
Silent Scope

AMERICAN ARCADE

Astroll's *American Arcade* is one of those retro-games like *PacMan* and *Frogger*. Old-school-type arcade game pinball machines, bowling, golf, gun range shooting, and fortune telling all make their appearances. It sounds sort of like an electronic carnival or State Fair Midway-area.

There are two types of modes: "Free," where you can play as long as you want; or "Challenge," where you get one credit to see how good you really are. It all takes you on a journey back to the classic arcade-style pinball machines.

GAUNTLET: DARK LEGACY

Midway Home Entertainment brings the follow-up to the hit revamp of everyone's favorite hack-and-slash dungeon crawler, *Gauntlet. Dark Legacy* ups the ante with four new main character classes (Sorceress, Dwarf, Jester, and Knight) to join the pre-existing four (Warrior, Wizard, Archer, and Valkyrie).

And there are four new worlds, in addition to the four old ones. For your gaming pleasure, all the endless swarms of enemies and RPG story elements are back.

SILENT SCOPE

In movies, it's usually the fifty-man SWAT team that takes down a terrorist enclave. Then again, there are times when only one person, a sniper rifle, and a box full of bullets will do. *Silent Scope*, another Konami title, makes you the sniper with a tireless arm, and a clock incessantly ticking away the minutes.

What's your mission, you ask? Clean out an entire city rife with terrorist threats. From rooftops to bridges, no one can escape your eagle eye. You hunt for your enemy's base in skyscrapers, hotels, and stadiums.

Silent Scope features different play levels from beginner to expert, and a night vision scope for night-time terrorist tracking, as well as three different game modes:

*Time attack: Here you compete to clear a stage fast with the highest accuracy all under an allotted amount of time.

*Story mode: The game proceeds as the story unfolds.

*Target practice: Hone your shooting skills with target practice.

Because you're up against the clock, the more time it takes for you to snipe someone, the less time you'll have in action on the next level. Yikes!

Look at www.konami-arcade.com/Arcade/SilentScope for more details and movies.

CLASSIC AND PUZZLE

Classic and puzzle games include puzzlers, board, mahjong, and shogi.

*AI Igo 2001
*AI Mahjong 2001
*AI Shogi 2001
*Fantavision
*I.Q. Remix +: Intelligent Qube
*Kakinoki Shogi IV
*Mahjong TaiKai III Millenium League
*Morita Shogi
*Shanghai 5

AL IGO 2001

Similar to *Othello*, 14 is bringing this rendition of the popular Japanese board game, *Go*. The game uses black and white stones on a checkerboard, but you land on the line intersections, not the squares.

AL MAHJONG 2001

Console mahjong. Mahjong is traditionally a tile game played by four players with 144 tiles that are drawn and discarded until one player secures a winning hand.

AL SHOGI 2001

Chess! However, there are some differences from chess, the most significant being the drop where you add a captured piece to your army in an empty square.

FANTAVISION

Fantavision, from Sony, is not what you think it might be. Critics have called it a glorified particle demo, but *Fantavision* actually proves to be a good puzzler, better than the *Tetris* revision for the PSX.

In order to score points you must catch launched fireworks in the air before they explode, and successfully detonate them. Ouch! Look out when catching them! There are three different colors of fireworks, and you have to catch at least three of the same colored fireworks to detonate them.

To get extra points, you need to catch a special rainbow-colored firework, and daisy-chain multiple fireworks of any color combination. However, your score drops if the launched fireworks fade before you can catch them.

Highly detailed backgrounds which move into space from earth, and hundreds of independently moving particles of the 3D fireworks explode in real-time.

I. Q. REMIX+: INTELLIGENT QUBE

This is the sequel to the puzzler game *Intelligent Qube* by Sony and Sugar & Rockets (www.scei.co.jp/sd2/iqr/index.html). Your role is that of a humanoid in an entirely purgatorial standing on a long marble row of gigantic blocks, with another collection of gigantic blocks on top of them that would, in sequence, tumble in your direction.

In the original *I.Q.*, your only defense was to set a bomb, clearing whatever colored cubes you could while avoiding the black forbidden cubes. If you hit a forbidden cube, any blocks you were working on would avalanche and tumble off the edge, and you'd lose a vertical row of blocks, making your working space a little smaller. To even things out, there were also green advantages—hitting one of these cubes resulted in the one-time use of a detonation field exactly one block long in every direction from where the advantage cube was hit. These would clear spaces so large that it would normally take at least nine hits to clear the same amount of space.

The new *I.Q.* premise is identical to the old except the graphics are better and there are two added views, including a third-person close-up.

KAKINOKI SHOGI IV

PlayStation2's processor is not just for complicated graphics and rapid action, but can be used for thinking routines. With this processor a better, faster shogi game can be created. The best to date, by Ascii Entertainment (www.scei.co.jp/cgi-bin/title.cgi?pnum=slps20004), is *Kakinoki Shogi IV*.

What's the secret? you may be asking. Well, the processor (CPU) thinks about the next move as you are thinking about your current move. So, by the time you play your move, the CPU has counter moves available for it. If you want to you can set a time limit for how long you'll allow the CPU to think, when the time expires, it plays the best move it has available. A perfect game for improving your own skill level.

Mahjong TaiKai III Millenium League

This mahjong game, developed by Koei (www.koei.co.jp/products/ee/Rlmarjan3.htm), is the PS2 sequel to the Dreamcast game, and features full-voice dialogue in addition to highly detailed opponent characters. 3D polygonal characters are used for each player, and it even includes several CG movies at the beginning of the game. There are several voice-overs as well, which may help make the game of mahjong more lively than ever.

Included is a tutorial section that teaches beginners what mahjong is all about, from the name of each block to the game rules. These narrated, interactive tutorials are great for newcomers.

Morita Shogi

Another sequel situation. *Morita Shogi* is the sequel to the N64 game, although shogi pro Kazuro Morita is assisting in the development with Yuki Enterprise (www.scei.co.jp/cgi-bin/title.cgi?pnum=slps20008). The PS2 version of *Morita Shogi* is approximately fifty times more intelligent then the original version.

In this version, there will be two modes: an instruction mode for the novice to get the hang of the basic strategies, and an assistant mode to help you plan your next move if you get road blocked and can't make a move.

SHANGHAI 5

This is the traditional Chinese board/tile game which is a version of solitaire. It uses the same tiles as mahjong, but stacked in an array. The object is to clear the board by matching pairs of free tiles. You can play this alone, or against another player.

DRIVING, RACING AND VEHICULAR COMBAT

What would the PlayStation2 be without car races, crashes, and general assault from within cars. There are plenty to choose from, and your choices ranges from auto, motor-cycle, fantasy, or vehicular combat.

*3D Real Drive
*Battle on the Ghat
*Choro Q HG
*Driving Emotion Type-S
*Evo Rally
*F1 2001
*F1 Racing Championship
*Ferrari 360 Challenge
*Ferrari Formula 1
*Formula One 2000
*Formula X
*Fusion GT
*The Getaway
*Gran Turismo 2000
*Midnight Club: Street Racing

*Moto GP
*Motor Mahem
*NASCAR 2001
*Rally Hard
*Ridge Racer V
*Road Rash
*Roadsters Trophy 2000
*Smuggler's Run
*Spin Sprint Car Racing
*Star Wars: Super Bombad Racing
*Street Lethal
*Wipeout Fusion
*World Destruction League: Thunder Tanks
*World Sports Cars

DRIVING EMOTION TYPE-S

Definitely a different driving game. Squaresoft and Escape (http://web.square.co.jp/gamefan/squaresoft/ps2/types/index2.html) have brought you amazing visuals with cars galore: Honda, Acura, Mazda, Toyota, Mitsubishi, Nissan, Alfa, BMW, and TVR, and all complete with authentically modeled interiors. Now if only they'd have a selection to let you G the car out . . .

For people who need practice, there is a full driving school available which offers training in cornering, accelerating, and braking, along with some advanced techniques for the more experienced drivers.

Driving Emotion Type-S

F1 RACING CHAMPIONSHIP

Ubi Soft (www.ubisoft.com/usa) is releasing *F1 Racing Championship*. It's more of a racing simulation game then an arcade, but you have a choice. The arcade game has a "pick-up-and-play" mode that keeps score, and offers bonus points depending on how rapidly you plow through the timed segments of each track and how many cars you've overtaken.

The timing areas even act as checkpoints that you have to pass through in an ever decreasing amount of time if you're to make it around all five laps. Finish in the top six and you move on to the next, harder track.

FERRARI 360 CHALLENGE

Acclaim (www.acclaim.com) brings you *Ferrari 360 Challenge*, the first PlayStation2 title to bear the moniker of the company's prized Ferrari license. While this game is the same as Sega's *F355 Challenge*, it veers away from the arcade-like elements of *Ridge Racer V*.

360 Challenge keeps the action centered in the real world, including physics, and handling, and the 360 will be the only car in the game, since developers Brain in a Jar have decided to focus on perfecting the different types of enemy racer AI. Driving choices range from reckless to conservative, and everything in between. Like so many of the Next Gen racing games, the way you race affects your opponents style as well, so cutting a racer off may send them into a fit of rage, and you into the ditch, thanks to their personal vendetta. Talk about road rage!

THE GETAWAY

No, it's not the old Steve McQueen movie, or even the remake from a few years ago—this one's much cooler. As a retired bank robber gone straight, you suddenly find yourself returning to your old ways in order to save your son, who's been kidnapped by the mob. (Kinda like a PS2 version of the Nicholas Cage movie *Gone in 60 Seconds*.) High-speed chases and hi-tech graphics? Gimme the keys— I'm drivin'!

The Getaway

GRAN TURISMO 2000

Another racing game that shows incredibly realistic driving simulation. GT2K has a high frame rate that stays steady even with buildings, bridges, and highways lining the tracks. The replays in the game are cool, with road heat rising as an entourage of cars comes racing past you. The cool thing is that this game will really benefit from the Dual Shock 2's analog-sensitive buttons in terms of acceleration and braking.

Gran Turismo 2000

MIDNIGHT CLUB: STREET RACING

Midnight Club: Street Racing

You begin this game from Rockstar and Angel Studios (www.angelstudios.com/mc.html) as a taxi driver in a city late at night. You attempt to catch the Midnight Club as they zoom past you on their way towards a secret warehouse destination. If you succeed, you'll join the secret group of racers competing for each other's pink slips in the three game cities: Tokyo, London, and New York. There are no rules and no set path; just be the first to the finish line, that's all.

Using the "Joy Ride" mode allows you to learn the back streets and shortcuts, giving you an advantage when it comes to plotting advance strategy. Victories mean advancing up the club ranks and gaining new sets of wheels to trick out with the kickest equipment money can buy.

Moto GP

Similar to *Gran Turismo 2000*, this motorbike racing game by Namco (www.namco.com) features detailed tracks, environments, and backgrounds, and allows you to compete for more money to buy better bikes and upgrades. This game is known as *500 GP* in Japan.

NASCAR 2001

Another EA Sports (www.easports.com) title is *NASCAR 2001*. Like the real-life NASCAR racing events, the driving

NASCAR 2001

action in this new game is just as exhilarating. Again, the emphasis is on realism and this title also adds graphical detail and high frame rates.

Each car can sustain damage at several points, so no wreck is the same as the last, and they look incredibly realistic. How hard a car is hit affects the damage sustained from slightly skewed driving ability to a totally blown, flaming engine.

The game features many of your favorite drivers and courses from the 2000 NASCAR season. EA Sports has programmed in the driving personalities of the racers so it doesn't just stop at appearances.

RIDGE RACER V

Another Namco title for PS2 is *Ridge Racer V*, a 3D racing game. It's a visual cornucopia for Sony's new machine. The smoothness of the graphics have been achieved through the usage of Gouraud techniques and improved 3D polygon rendering power. (Gouraud shading is used for polygon approximations to curved surfaces, linear interpolation of intensity along scan lines, and eliminates the intensity of discontinuities at polygon edges.)

Ridge Racer V sports stages of landscapes reflected on the car bodies, and an immense range of lighting effects, plus tires smoking during hard braking and tail-slides. There are also shooting sparks when car bodies graze each other. The racecourse is detailed with shimmering heat waves, looming buildings, and an improved perspective on distance which make the game all the more real for players.

Check out www.namco.com/console/titles/ridge_racer_v.html for more information.

Ridge Racer V

ROAD RASH

Similar to road rage, EA (www.ea.com) created *Road Rash* which is part of a series developed for all consoles, PCs, and GameBoy. You race your bike on a selection of five different tracks, and then knock your opponents off their bikes using your fists, legs, or weapons. Get to the finish line first to win some big money. Use your prize money to buy a better motorcycle.

ROADSTERS TROPHY 2000

Titus (www.titusgames.com/indexFlash.html) is currently developing the sequel to the *Roadsters* game created for the Japanese PS2. It will simulate racing luxury convertible cars with changing weather conditions and accurate vehicle handling. In order to stay in the lead you need to purchase cars and upgrades. Trading cars and betting them will be another way to gain leverage.

SMUGGLER'S RUN

Ever thought about trying to outrun the law? Well, get that thought right out of your head this instant, mister! Crime doesn't pay!

Actually, though, crime can be fun—at least in the world of videogaming. In Angel Studios' *Smuggler's Run*—published by Rockstar—your objective is to smuggle (duh!) unnamed contraband across four tough environments: jungles, forests, snowy tundra, and blazing hot deserts. But don't worry—you're not expected to do it in the latest Saturn or Volkswagen; no, you get to tear across the countryside in a collection of four-by-four vehicles. After all, being a smuggler, a normal, paved road is the last place you want to drive—especially with the police waiting for you at every turn!

STREET LETHAL

Have you ever gone to one of those auto shows and seen those weird, kinda futuristic-looking cars—things that look like they came straight outta *Blade Runner*? Well, those are what are known as "concept cars," mainly because they never get produced beyond the prototype display model. You've probably always wondered what it'd be like to drive one of those bad boys, right?

Wonder no longer, friends. Through the efforts of the fine folks at Exackt Entertainment, not only does their game *Street Lethal* put you behind the wheel of an array of

Street Lethal

concept cars, but you can even design your own racing machines, too! The streets and freeways of ten international cities—including Paris, London, and Los Angeles—will be your race courses, and the game's publisher, Activision, has announced that *Street Lethal* will include secret cars and courses, 2-on-2 racing (so your friends can eat your dust), real-time car damage, and an advanced opponent AI.

WIPEOUT FUSION

In the game, the year is 2150 AD, and the Federation has unveiled the next generation of racing craft that will allow for a more advanced level of maneuverability.

The original *Wipeout's* crafts only featured seven parameters to define the ship's handling, but the ships found in *Wipeout Fusion* will offer *forty-eight* parameters. The ships are also capable of true antigravity maneuvers—you can now race upside down on tracks or at any angle you choose.

Psygnosis, which is owned by Sony (www.sony.com), is trying to make the racing sport more attractive to new fans. The Federation has selected a wide range of racing venues, each with its own new interactive features and some with freeform areas that don't limit pilots to just following the track. Courses will be more interactive, and you'll have a wider array of navigation decisions to make. Additionally, there will be a more powerful and diverse arsenal of weapons.

Wipeout Fusion

FIGHTING

Who would want to miss a good videogame fight—or miss competing in one? Here are some electronic ways to vent your aggressions with a handy dose of console assault & battery.

*Baki the Grappler
*Bloody Roar 3
*The Bouncer
*Dead or Alive 2
*Dynasty Warriors 2
*Kengo: Master of Bushido
*Kensetsu Juuki Kenka Battle Buchigire Kongou!!
*Street Fighter EX 3
*Tekken Tag Tournament
*WCW 2001

BAKI THE GRAPPLER

Based on manga and animé character *Grappler Baki*, the ultimate fighter who has an innate sixth sense about the strengths and weaknesses of his opponents, Tomy Entertainment brings Baki Hanma to the console wrestling environment.

BLOODY ROAR 3

This title by Hudson Soft continues the *Bloody Roar* series of 3D fighting games where you can morph into a half human/half animal creature, like a Centaur. After changing into the beast, you have more power and can wreck lots more havoc on your opponents.

THE BOUNCER

Matrix-style freeze-and-spin panning effects, as well as intriguing environment interaction. There are dazzling cut-scenes, with realistically modeled bestial humans, detailed urban simulation, and full voice acting.

Square (www.playonline.com) are the masters of adventure game-making, and *The Bouncer* incorporates this skill into a hybrid fighting/adventure type game using a four-person fighting system in which your players form a gang that rampage through various scenes. The battles are fully 3D and interactive, with lots of room to roam in the fight and special effects, including explosions equivalent to a Hollywood film.

The Bouncer promises to be a cross between a story-driven action/adventure game and a classic fighter.

The Bouncer

DEAD OR ALIVE 2

While not as popular as *Tekken* or *Street Fighter*, the original *Dead or Alive* by Tecmo (www.tecmo.co.jp/product/doa/doa_home.htm) was often considered fundamentally complex by hardcore fighting fans, thanks to its reversal and block system, and many critics dismissed the game as nothing more than a showcase for huge-breasted women and the effect that the laws of physics have on their chests in a fight. However, those who saw past this obvious adolescent selling point discovered what was often thought of as one of the best fighting games to be released in recent years.

DOA2 boasts over seventy-five million polygons, and features levels that are often multi-tiered. The additional polygons improve the motions of characters' faces as they talk with one another. There are also a ton of extra options that can't be found anywhere else, including more costumes and more intense lighting.

Dead or Alive 2

DYNASTY WARRIORS 2

Created by the Omega-Force team (www.koei.co.jp/
products/ee/new/musou2/musou2.htm), *Dynasty Warriors*
2 makes it possible for players to experience the valor of
the combatants from the popular game series that introduced the "Romance of the Three Kingdoms" saga.

In DW2, the most minute character movements are
detailed in a true 3D environment. Strategy plays a criti-
cal role in the gameplay: You must find the weaknesses of
your enemy's encampment, and make sure you are well
defended to vanquish them.

KENGO: MASTER OF BUSHIDO

Lightweight, the team behind the *Bushido Blade* games,
returns to the way of the Samurai. Featured are aspects of

the true, stark, and decisive fighting that made the *Bushido Blade* series so popular, but with multiple opponents getting in the way of your curved blade.

As you climb the ranks of the elite Zen warriors, your skill level increases, and you get a chance to enter the Emperor's tournament to prove your prowess. If you were a fans of the cleanly delineated action of *Bushido Blade*, then you need to check this out.

KENSETSU JUUKI KENKA BATTLE BUCHIGIRE KONGOU!!

A 3D fighting game from Artdink (www.artdink.co.jp/japanese/special/spe10.html), *Buchigire Kongou* is a game where the character you play is a construction worker. You simply get in a construction vehicle (for example, a front-end loader) and battle head-to-head with someone else's construction vehicle (like a bulldozer) on a 3D battlefield. Very soothing, especially if you're irritated at a contractor.

STREET FIGHTER EX 3

This is the third installment of the *Street Fighter EX* series, but in 3D fighting format, created by Capcom (www.capcom.com) and developer Arika with most of the same fighters, plus a few new ones not seen in prior games.

This sequel allows you to select two characters to tag team fight. Other new features include the "Dramatic Battle," where you fight 1-on-2 or 1-on-3, and "Team Battle," where you can select up to five members to go against your opponent.

One of the biggest differences in gameplay over the regular 2D *Street Fighter* games is that you can chain super-combos together. Chaining hits together can lead to big points!

Street Fighter EX3

Tekken Tag Tournament

One of the first releases in Japan, and an arcade game series since 1994, the new console version of *TTG* for PS2 features at least twenty fighters who have appeared throughout the *Tekken* series. The fighters look like CG characters, but they are all real-time.

The new console version has astounding detail. There is a tropical island stage that is covered with endless blades of grass, weeds, and other plants that move with the wind, or when characters walk by. Another level displays buildings and glaring neon signs reflected in the wet streets, which must be an update of Lei's Chinatown.

Check out www.namco.com/console/titles/tekken_tag_tournament.html for more information.

Tekken Tag Tournament

ROLE-PLAYING

Role-playing isn't for everyone, but diehards from the *Dungeons & Dragons* clubs days will get into these games, and some of them are pretty cool, even if you aren't a role player.

*Baldur's Gate Legends
*Boku To Maoh
*Dark Cloud
*Ephemeral Phantasia
*Eternal Blade
*Eternal Ring
*Evergrace
*Final Fantasy X
*Final Fantasy XI
*Jade Cocoon 2
*The John Woo/Chow Yun-Fat Project
*Legion: Legend of Excalibur
*One/fourth
*Orphen: Sorcerous Stabber
*Popolocrois III
*Reiselied Ephemeral Fantasia

*Soldnerschild 2
*Star Ocean 3
*Suikoden III
*Summoner
*Symphony of Light

BALDUR'S GATE LEGENDS

Interplay (www.interplay.com) shocked the RPG community by not announcing a port of the PC blockbuster *Baldur's Gate* for PlayStation2, but rather an entirely new 3D adventure game entitled *Baldur's Gate Legends*.

In case you don't know the previous *Baldur's Gate* games, they essentially bring *Advanced Dungeons & Dragons* to the computer. You can immerse yourself in the medieval fantasy world of the Forgotten Realms, where nations hang in the balance of your actions, dark prophecies test your perseverance, and heroic dreams can, at last, be fulfilled.

Planning to dump the static 2D rendered graphics of its PC predecessor, Legends re-creates the Forgotten Realms world in full polygonal splendor for the first time.

DARK CLOUD

Dark Cloud by Level 5 (www.level5.co.jp/darktitle.htm) puts you in a world where the title vaporous antagonist has imprisoned and transformed every living being on the planet. For mysterious reasons, you are the only one spared, and you must single-handedly rebuild the world.

Little is known about how the game's completely innovative "georama" system—which allows you to build entire sections of a world, and then hop into it seamlessly in real-time—will be used. The system, though, is similar to Square's *Legend of Mana*, where you can use objects to create entire worlds, but the difference lies in the fact that *Legend of Mana* is not in real-time.

Dark Cloud

ETERNAL RING

Are you a *King's Field* fan? Well, here you go. *Eternal Ring* by From Software (www.fromsoftware.co.jp/soft/er/er/main.html) borrows from the methodical style of *King's Field* games, but *Eternal Ring* is unique in its approach to conveying the story.

Eternal Ring tells the story of Kain Morgan, a man with the ability to bring together elemental rings in order to form powerful spells. Kain's task is to venture to the Island of No Return, where he must slay eight dragons. Kain can command fire, ice, wind, lightning, water, light, and darkness when he combines the rings in various ways, and there are literally hundreds of rings.

EVERGRACE

Evergrace is also created by From Software (www.from software.co.jp/soft/eg/eg/index.html) and is the company's second 3D-action RPG offering. In *Evergrace* you have the option of controlling one of two characters throughout the game: a swordsman, or an archer.

Evergrace benefits from the advantages of the DVD format in that it includes plenty of voice acting throughout the game, and—thanks to the larger storage space— textures for all the different characters' equipment and items can be stored on the discs. That way, when you change armor you'll be able to see the differences. Neither adventurer interacts with the other, and each has a unique storyline which will double the game's replay value and length.

FINAL FANTASY X

Square (http://web.square.co.jp) presents its first PlayStation2 *Final Fantasy* game. *Final Fantasy X* will offer a whole new angle to the always altering FF universe. The latest game in the series will have almost nothing to do with previous games, but Square's PlayOnline plans on helping you out, in order to provide a more enjoyable game play.

Although not fully integrated (like its follow-up, *Final Fantasy XI*), Square states that if you're playing *Final Fantasy X* you will be able to seamlessly switch between the game and PlayOnline's resources, dashing into a chat room to ask some questions before proceeding.

Final Fantasy XI

Final Fantasy XI further expands the online environment for gaming. Square has been watching the huge successes of online multi-player role-playing games like *Everquest, Asheron's Call*, and *Ultima Online*, and decided to release *Final Fantasy XI* as an online-only RPG experience.

Final Fantasy XI

Square's proprietary online service, PlayOnline, will house the game servers and encourage thousands of simultaneous users to play the game, chat in real-time, or shop. PlayOnline plans to be a worldwide service, offering players from Asia, Europe, and North and South America to play together via any broadband connection and a PlayStation2.

The John Woo/Chow Yun-Fat Project

No, that's not the actual title, but at the time of this book's printing, this upcoming RPG doesn't have one yet. The bottom line is Sony is currently developing a game that would combine the ballet-like gun battle of action movie director John Woo (*Face/Off, Broken Arrow, Mission: Impossible 2*) with the kind of brooding, quasi-heroic characters portrayed by actor Chow Yun-Fat (*The Replacement Killers*). Expect to see lots of characters leaping through the air, both guns blazing, while flocks of doves fly across the background.

The untitled shoot-'em-up is planned for release sometime in 2002.

ORPHEN: SORCEROUS STABBER

Questing for the golden prophet, the protagonists of *Orphen: Sorcerous Stabber* end up on the mysterious Chaos Island. Three different storylines intertwine, each one unique. Activision (www.activision.com) and Shade have created delicious environments that include gigantic castles, underground caves, and dark forests. Over thirty different monsters and nine bosses oppose you, while you advance through the levels by running, jumping, and climbing. Included are puzzles and secrets, along with anime sequence enhancement.

POPOLOCROIS III

Popolocrois II

SCEA is offering the third game in the *Popolocrois* series. This version of its strange, yet oddly compelling role-playing series features a unique visual style that blends cartoon-like character designs with 3D polygonal models. The result is something that looks sort of like *Fear Effect* for the PSX, only much more convincing and graphically rich.

Maybe SCEA will localize this game since it has such a huge following outside of North America.

SUIKODEN III

One of the most popular RPG series created for the original PlayStation has been Konami's *Suikoden* series, so it only makes sense that the company has announced plans for a PS2 game. Konami, however, is keeping mum about the game's new features and technological specs; they'll only say (at the time of this printing) that the game will be released in Japan by fall 2001.

SUMMONER

Summoner (www.summoner.com) is an upcoming fantasy RPG from PC developers Volition, who previously succeeded with *Descent: Freespace*, and then again with *Freespace 2*.

Volition wants to "wow" their gamers with the most original and stunning RPGs to ever be shown on a console. With *Summoner*, you're placed in the shoes of Joseph, a young man who has the power to summon, by using rings, demons to golems.

SIMULATION

Simulation games are about creating a virtual world within a game that you control. You interact with the virtual world and see your actions take effect in the game. Some examples of simulated environments include virtual communities, flight simulation, and musical rhythm games.

Particularly popular on the PS2 are the music and dance simulation titles. The subject matter is lighter, no virtual community residents die if you miss a beat, and if you follow the groove you'll have a lot of fun.

*A6: A Ressha de Ikou 6
*BBD 2000
*Bust A Move 3
*Densha De Go!
*Dream Audition
*DrumMania
*EX Japan Special Express
*FX Pilot
*L'Arc~en~Ciel
*Panzer Century G Breaker
*Pilot ni Narou! 2

*Primal Image Vol. 1
*Rockin' Mega Stage
*Sidewinder Max
*Sim Theme Park
*Stepping Selection
*TVDJ
*Typhoon
*Unison
*World Neverland 3

A6: A Ressha de Ikou 6

Artdink (www.jp.playstation.com/cgi-bin/ncommerce3/ Product-Display?prmenbr=3511&prrfnbr=24562) created this sixth game in the series, also known as *A-Train 6*. The premise is that you control the construction and development of a city railway transportation system similar to all the previous A-Trains, but now the city will react in real time.

If you run the rail system efficiently, the city will progress on its own, using an "emotional city" growth system. Details of the moving, growing city are very intricate, with everything changing in relation to the health of your rail system.

Bust a Move 3

This makes a trilogy of Japanese musical mix-and-dance competition games developed by Enix (www.enix.co.jp). *Bust A Move 3* (its Japanese title) will most likely will be re-titled to *Bust A Groove 3* for the North American and European release, in keeping with the two previous releases in this popular series.

Densha De Go!

Another train simulation game title, this one by Taito. Those Japanese sure do like trains—the title means "Go by train!"

Apparently there are a lot of train enthusiasts who have been chomping at the bit to be able to drive a commuter train of their own. The gameplay basically consists of switching gears, increasing and decreasing speed, and being able to stop at the station without passing the lone passenger on the platform.

It seems like you're in a straight line the whole way. There are four different tracks you can drive on, with different graphics for all. The graphics are cool—they look like they're digitized photos of Japanese towns.

DrumMania

Originally released as an arcade game, *DrumMania* is another game in Konami's Bemani series (also known as *Beatmania*). Like previous music games, *DrumMania* gives you the opportunity to get into the rhythm with several musical pieces by pressing a number of buttons at correct intervals and playing music with the rest of the song or tune.

This game comes with a special controller that consists of three drums, two cymbals, and a foot pedal. A variety of musical genres is included in the game such as j-pop, rock, and blues. Up to three players can join in by using the guitar or Dual Shock controllers.

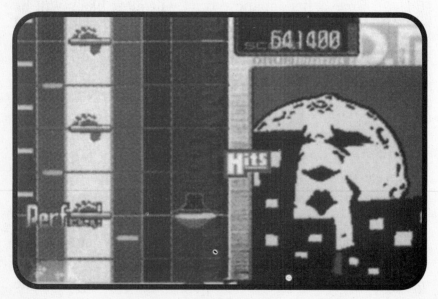

DrumMania

PRIMAL IMAGE VOL. 1

Developed by Atlus (www.atlus.co.jp/cs/new/primal.htm), *Primal Image* promises to be one of the most unusual—and voyueristic—games ever created for the PS2. The deal is that you're a fashion photographer, and your goal is to take sexy snapshots of young and beautiful models. You can choose one of four CG models, and choose a behavior type for your photo session.

Primal Image Vol. 1

Once the photo shoot starts, you take snapshots at different, random camera angles; at the end of the session, you see thumbnails of your pictures. The game tallies (referred to as "bits") up your score based on how sexy your pictures are, and that's it. And no, you can't save the pictures to your memory card.

SIM THEME PARK

A fun day at the theme park: Waiting in long lines only to go on a very short ride, paying too much money for bad food, and then getting sick on the pavement—EA has ported all the real-world aspects of a day at an amusement park to the PlayStation2. You control all aspects of the park, from constructing the rides to salting the fries. Balance the fun and profitability of the park by testing out the rides in full 3D splendor.

Not enough for you? How about dropping into the shoes of some of your patrons to explore the park's 128-bit 3D decadence. Snag some cotton candy, munch on a bag of popcorn, or just take a gander at how large that super-coaster you bought really is. Or try hopping on one of your roller coasters or taking a ride around a park-wide log jam.

SimTheme Park allows you to build, and ride blood-curdling five-loop roller coasters in the most realistic way. Have fun.

STEPPING SELECTION

Retro game from Jaleco (www.jaleco.co.jp) that features hit songs from the '70s to today. You dance and match the steps. The music videos in the game feature their respective artists, such as Britney Spears and the Backstreet Boys. You can watch these videos in a separate mode without playing the actual game, and each CD-ROM will contain thirteen songs.

The game features a standard mode; a challenge mode, where players can change the difficulty of the game into four difficulty levels; an all-music mode, which lets players change songs; and two hidden modes only featured in the PS2 version: "Twin Mode" (for experts) and "License Mode." The menu on the game indicates an append-disc function, which means that add-ons may be released in the future. There are six buttons to press according to the rhythm and visual cues.

Stepping Selection is pretty pricey, though—the game contains two CDs, and the controller is sold separately for $61.00. Ouch!

TVDJ

Suddenly, you are the program director at a poor TV station, courtesy of Sony. In order to keep the sinking station afloat, you must edit and remix TV programs skillfully to increase viewer ratings.

Place one to four blocks of data in the right location at the correct time to properly remix the different segments. After completing the editing process, you can replay the entire sequence to view your completed masterpiece. If your TV show is edited well, your viewer ratings will increase, saving the TV station and keeping you out of the unemployment lines. But if your montage sucks, guess where you end up? In the poorhouse.

SPORTS

Definitely a big draw for most gaming fans are sports, and there's quite a lot of choices, too. Every nation has a favorite sport, and there are heated debates about what sports are best. So far, there are approximately thirty titles in the works for PS2, ranging from baseball to wrestling. These games benefit from the system's polygon power to render more realistic features on people, whether they be the audience or the competitors. As mentioned before, playing with two people is great, using the multi-tap and playing with four is ever better, but broadband—where you can get a whole team of people to play with—will be amazing. Of course, these offerings don't seem to be promising this, but just wait, it's right around the corner.

   *1 on 1 Government
   *All-Star Baseball 2002
   *All Star Pro Wrestling
   *Bakuyru 2
   *Doukyuu Billiards Master 2
   *ESPN International Track and Field
   *ESPN X Games: Snowboarding

*EX Billiards
*Gekikuukan Pro Baseball:
 The End of The Century 1999
*FIFA Soccer World Championship
*Jikkyou Powerful Pro Baseball 7
*Jikkyou World Soccer 2000
*Knockout Kings 2001
*Lakemasters EX
*Madden NFL 2001
*Magical Sport Go Go Golf
*Magical Sports 2000 Koshien
*Magical Sports Killer Bass 2
*NBA Live 2001
*NBA 2 Night
*NHL 2001
*NHL FaceOff 2001
*Perfect Golf 3
*Ready 2 Rumble: Round 2
*Snowboard SuperX
*Sky Surfer
*Sled Storm 2
*Stunt Squad
*Swing Away Golf
*This Is Football 2
*Tiger Woods PGA Tour 2001

ALL STAR BASEBALL 2002

Ah, baseball. America's Favorite Pastime. No surprise, then, that Acclaim has announced the forthcoming release of a PS2 sequel to their popular Nintendo 64 series. Among the features you can look forward to are six modes of play, three—count 'em!—three announcers, and the sort of highly detailed graphics that only the PS2 engine could

All Star Baseball 2002

deliver. All Major League ballparks will be included, modeled precisely on their real-world counterparts, and games will be played in daylight, at dusk, and under nighttime lighting. Batter up!

ALL STAR PRO WRESTLING

All Star Pro Wrestling is SquareSoft's (www.squaresoft.co.jp) answer to wrestling mania. Focusing on detail and substance

All Star Pro Wrestling

rather than flash, *ASP Wrestling* boasts one of the most detailed grappling engines in the genre. The sidelines are sparse, but the wrestler's skin ripples with exertion, which is way cool.

ESPN Internation Track and Field

Did you catch Olympic fever this past summer, while you were watching the games in Sydney, Australia? Well, if you haven't been able to shake that bug (or even if you don't want to), here's the kind of game that'll keep you dreaming of Olympic gold. From track events to swimming meets, *Track and Field* features shifting camera angles that'll make you think you're watching a live TV broadcast.

Hey, does that mean a PS2 version of *SportsCenter* comes on to give the game's highlights when you're finished playing?

FIFA Soccer World Championship

FIFA SOCCER WORLD CHAMPIONSHIP

FIFA Soccer World Championship is the only series allowed to use the World Cup theme because it is licensed by both FIFA (Federation Internationale de Football Association) in Zurich and the JFA (Japan Football Association).

EA Canada (www.japan.ea.com/archive/fifa2k_ps2/index.html) has made use of international soccer star Hidetoshi Nakata as the "image player," a function he performed in *FIFA '99*. The crowds are large, and all the athletes demonstrate life-like movements. In order to create these life-like movements, Nataka's actions were motion-captured, and all of his soccer techniques are rendered in the game, including kicks, passes, corner kicks, and overhead shots.

The game itself features nearly photo-realistic graphics and smooth animation. Other graphic touches include light-sourcing that produces accurate shadows from players on the field, and highly detailed crowd animation. Identical to previous games in the series, you will be able to play with the European Leagues as well.

Jikkyou Powerful Pro Baseball 7

Jikkyou Powerful Pro Baseball series has made an appearance on just about every console game ever made. Now, Konami is bringing it to the PlayStation2, with the same type of cartoony characters, but with better details and smoother appearances. Promised is a new evolution from the prior series, offering a new baseball experience.

Knockout Kings 2001

Knockout Kings 2001

As the name implies, this Black Ops Entertainment (www.blackops.com/main.htm) game is about boxing. All the egomaniacal violent splendor of heavyweight boxing comes to the PlayStation2. Stand up and holler! Ain't that great?

New CyberScan technology allows the boxers' faces to be accurately reproduced in full polygonal glory. The game also features new modes of play and simplified control as well. Choose your champion from a stable of boxing's greatest, including—you just gotta wear shades for this line-up—Muhammad Ali, Joe Louis, Rocky Marciano, and Lennox Lewis.

Dang! You even get a new "Career" mode that allows you to play through several weight classes, boxing at famous arenas around the world.

MADDEN NFL 2001

For this game, EA Sports (www.easports.com/games/madden2001/ps2.html) plans to recapture the market share of finger sports aficionados with the ultimate football sim. Download a movie to pique your curiosity at www.ps2.net.

Madden NFL 2001

A fandangled thing is "Madden Cards." You guessed it: a collectable card game and bonus unlocker. When you earn a card, you can hang on to it, use it to bump up your player's stats, or, if it's rare, put it on the line in a normal football game against a friend who's offering up some of his best cards, winner takes all. Cool graphics utilize the polygon power of the PS2. Helmets accurately reflect the immediate environment. NFL coaches also appear on-screen, realistically rendered using EA's Cyberscan technology.

NBA LIVE 2001

EA Sports brings its pop-ular basketball franchise to the PlayStation2 with *NBA Live 2001*. Visually, this game looks com-pletely different from anything seen before. EA's CyberScan technolo-gy has mapped the play-

NBA Live 2001

ers' faces with frightening accuracy.

Check out some of the EA games throughout this book—they've done a fine job of rendering whatever they are creating so that everything looks uncannily real. The players' faces, and the increased polygon count of the players' bodies, yield people who look almost too life-like. All the NBA stadiums are perfectly reproduced, and new camera angles show off the detailed polygonal constructs. Gameplay remains largely unchanged, with only minor tweaks to the already popular system, but you can control your player's appearance so that he looks exactly as you wish. This is a hot graphical game.

READY 2 RUMBLE: ROUND 2

Talk about just beating it! In this sequel to the vastly popular PlayStation game, developer Midway has added a special guest celebrity boxer—none other than the "King of Pop" himself, Michael Jackson! Seems the Gloved One is a huge fan of the original *R2R*, and he approached Midway about being included in the new version; he even went so far as to help them in motion-capturing his signature moves—including the "Moonwalk"—and providing voice samples.

Jacko's not the only big name included in the game, however. Basketball ace Shaquille O'Neal will also be featured, along with a few other celebrities whose identities, at this time, have yet to be revealed.

SNOWBOARD SUPERX

Electronics Arts (http://ssx.ea.com) is bringing on *Snowboard SuperX* (pronounced "super-cross"), a 3D snowboard racing game. Its design focuses on simulating real routes and snowboard physics. Added is an international feel because both courses and characters are from around the world. You may even find an Italian taunting you in the native language.

Gameplay modes focus on different elements, like performing tricks or racing for time. Tricks are tracked on an adrenaline bar, which means that the better your tricks, the more adrenaline you get—just like in real-life snowboarding! Characters have 5000 polygons (twice the Japanese version) and you see them with dynamic camera views. There will also be four-player multi-tap support.

SKY SURFER

ESPN brought sky surfing to the television, and now Idea Factory is bringing it to the PS2. In this game, there are two modes: Training and Competition. You can practice your moves in a wind chamber in the training mode, and you can take your skills and run for the skies in competition mode.

SWING AWAY GOLF

EA (www.scei.co.jp/cgi-bin/title.cgi?pnum=slps20009) has picked this cute golf simulation in the vein of *Hot Shots Golf*. The game features cartoon-like characters swinging their clubs through finely detailed polygonal courses, and the physics engine is surprisingly realistic. You get up to four players to compete with, in a variety of modes, and the gameplay is quick and easy to understand.

TIGER WOODS PGA TOUR 2001

Tiger Woods—who else could win the British Open? Amazing. Before Tiger came to the game I thought it was boring, but his spunk enlivened the glowing televised event for me. Now, EA Sports brings the energy and sportsmanship of Tiger to the first PGA licensed game for this system. Tiger joins a large group of other PGA stars available for the choosing in this game. Select your poison and take to the greens of Pebble Beach, SpyGlass Hill, or Poppy Hills.

And check out that swing interface! It's new, using the analog controller to control the power and speed of your swing. Realistic graphics render the courses in full 3D splendor, creating the most life-like golf environment ever seen in console gameland.

STRATEGY

You have to use your brain for strategy games, but even though you have to think, there still is a plethora of killing, pillaging, and destruction to keep your adrenaline rushing, and your hands aching.

*Age of Empires II: The Age of Kings
*Chin Wen No Sangokushi
*Dropship
*Evolva
*FantaVision
*Ghost Master
*Hidden and Dangerous 2
*ICO
*Kessen
*Legion: Legend of Excalibur
*Nooks and Crannies
*Pirates of Skull Cove
*Red
*The Dreamland Chronicles: Freedom Ridge
*War Monkeys

AGE OF EMPIRES II: THE AGE OF KINGS

Konami is bringing Microsoft's single-player campaigner *Age of Empires* to the PS2, and Age of Kings was one of the best-selling real-time PC strategy games of 1999. *Kings* follows the campaigns of famous historical heroes such as Joan of Arc and William

Age of Empires II: The Age of Kings

Wallace. Each of the thirteen civilizations included in the game come with their own spoken language and unique unit.

THE DREAMLAND CHRONICLES: FREEDOM RIDGE

Mythos Games (www.mythos.com/pp) brings the *Dreamland Chronicles*, where you control the Terran Liberation Army against alien invaders in a strategy RPG-style game set in the near future of Earth. The action will take place in both third- and first-person perspectives, and will probably be similar to an earlier Mythos creation, *X-Com*.

EVOLVA

The goal in this game is to take on the role of one of the Evolva—elite commanders—then take a group of genetically-engineered warriors called Genohunters and mutate, change, and evolve them to the point where they can be used to defeat a deadly alien parasite threatening the planet. Genohunters are incredibly adaptive because they evolve by absorbing the remains of enemies and mutating themselves to incorporate the dead's useful abilities after analyzing their DNA.

Computer Artwork is porting the PC game to the PS2. Check out www.interplay.com/evolva for screenshots and tons of Evolva information.

GHOST MASTER

Empire Interactive (www.empire.co.uk) brings this mix of real-time strategy and haunted house hijinks. You assume the role of the local Ghost Master, a spirit who must cleanse the area of human activity. No *Casper the Friendly Ghost* here, but *Scooby Doo* fans will enjoy this kitschy little piece. You use psychic powers to create monsters and ghosts that drive the humans away.

ICO

This puzzler, offered by SCEA, features a young boy who must venture into a castle filled with traps to rescue a princess who's had a spell placed on her. The princess can't see well, and as a result, she needs the boy to help her navigate the castle's many traps and pitfalls in order to make it to safety.

The adventure and puzzle-solving elements, as well as an intuitive third-person camera, make this an exciting game. The cool thing is that the camera is normally stationary, but you have the option to unlock it and move it around.

KESSEN

Kessen, a Japanese feudal war sim by Keoi (www.koei.co.jp/products/ee/new/kessen/kessen.htm), is a console revolution in real-time strategy. Incredible large-scale epic battles that move fluidly—played out in real-time—and hundreds of large-scale soldiers that can be focused on, offering a view of large armies colliding in combat. Or pull the camera back to see thousands of units sprawled across the countryside.

Included is in-depth historical coverage, since this game is based on real situations involving famous warriors.

NOOKS AND CRANNIES

Taking place in the year 2509 AD, *Nooks and Crannies* places you in control of two new species: the Nooks and the Crannies that live in an uncharted galaxy. Both creatures have sour dispositions and notoriously short fuses, changing from mild annoyance to flipping murderous rage faster then you can blink. They are jealous, selfish and violent, and will kill each other over the slightest provocation. This is a good thing because they multiply faster then rabbits.

Bonus! Each copy of *Nooks and Crannies* contains the DNA of a unique creature that you must develop and breed. You can even email different strands of DNA you've created to friends to increase the fun. And if that wasn't exciting enough, the game's developer, AndNow (www.andnow.net/nooks/index.html), will also feature special DNA and other cool downloads on its Web site.

RED

Red appears to be another Japanese fighting game—yes, this is a military war sim, but it's set in an alternate reality where Japan has been split into three separate territories after World War II.

The bottom line with this game by Konami is that, besides turn-based and real-time strategy elements, you have the opportunity to command big, hulking mecha around war-torn Japan.

WAR MONKEYS

In the year 2161, on the planet Primus IV, three opposing forces engage in war. Silicon Dreams (www.sdreams.co.uk) created this 3D environment that displays up to 200 individuals simultaneously and renders a battlefield of up to 25 kilometers. That's almost fifteen miles! You can even improve your army's strengths and capabilities instead of mass-producing expendable units.

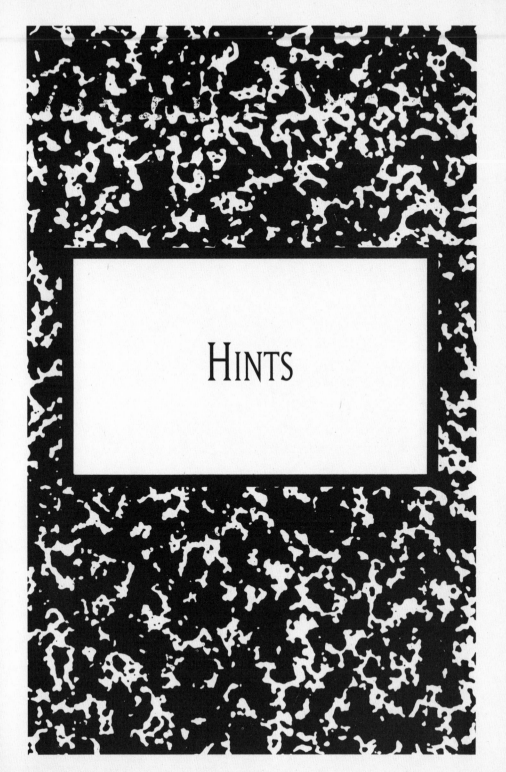

HINTS

D on't have the patience to figure out the intricacies of every level of every game coming your way? Then here, on the proverbial silver platter, are cheats for some of the hottest, kicking games spinning on the PlayStation2. Make sure you check out the Web site section, because plenty of sites list cheats, hints, tips, and tricks for all those confusing levels.

ARMORED CORE 2

First Person View: During gameplay, hold Triangle + Square + Start. The game will now be paused. Press "Start" to resume gameplay with a new camera view. For the Japanese version, hold Triangle + Square + Select.

Fixed Camera View: During gameplay, hold Circle + X + Start. The game will now be paused. Press "Start" to resume game play in a fixed camera view. For the Japanese version, hold Circle + X + Select.

Default View: What? You want to go back to the default view? Pause the game and press "Start" to resume the game with the original view. For the Japanese version, just press "Select."

DEAD OR ALIVE 2

Probably the most talked about—and unusual—aspects of the first *Dead or Alive* fighting game was its "bounce effect," in which the (sizable) chests of the female fighters rebounded in relation to the characters' movements.

In order to do the "bounce trick" in DOA 2, go to the options sub-menu "Other." The age you enter there determines how buoyant the chicks are—the higher your age, the . . . er, bouncier they become.

DRUM MANIA

To enable the guitar modes, enter the following commands at the "Mode Select" screen.

The legend is: R = Red, G = Green, B = Blue, P = Pink
• **Fast Flow:** R, G, B, P, P
• **Super Fast Flow:** R, G, B, P, P, R, G, B, P, P
• **Hidden:** R, B, G, B, R, G
• **Blank Screen:** R, B, G, B, R, G, R, B, G, B, R, G
• **Random:** B, G, G, R, G, P

There are several hidden modes. Perform the following drum sequences to activate the following:
• **Expert:** Hi-Hat, Hi-Hat, Snare, Snare, High Tom, Low Tom, High Tom, Bass, Bass
• **Mirror:** Snare, Snare, High Tom, Low Tom, High Tom, Bass
• **Hidden:** Low Tom, High Tom, Low Tom, High Tom, Low Tom, Bass
• **Speed Up:** Hi-Hat, Snare, Hi-Hat, Hi-Hat, Snare, Hi-Hat, Bass

RIDGE RACER V

In order to unlock the "Duel" mode, you must place first in both Lap and Overall Time in the Standard Time Attack GP. Once you're in "Duel" mode, you can unlock secret cars by winning the races. You can use these new cars in the Duel, Time Attack, and Free Run modes:
• Danver Spectra-50's super drift Cadillac
• Kamata Angelus-McLaren F1 ripoff with best top speed
• Rivelta Crinale-Devil drift car
• Solort Rumeur-Modern day VW Bug with super-grip handling

To use the third-person view onscreen display, hold Select while racing in the third-person perspective to display onscreen information that includes the amount of pressure being used on various controller buttons.

If you want to control the introduction sequence, start by pressing L1 and R1 during the introduction to cycle through three different effects for the portion that uses the in-game graphics. Press R1 for black and white graphics. Press R1 a second time, and the graphics will have a yellow tint. Press R1 a third time to add blur effect, which eliminates jagged graphics. Press L1 to cycle back through the various effects.

SKY SURFER
The myriad of trick moves include:
- **Scorpion:** Circle, Triangle, X
- **Menhouse Surprise:** Square, Triangle, X
- **Opening Touring Car:** Square, Square, Square, Circle
- **The Plate:** Triangle, X Triangle, X
- **Tidy Bowl in the Hole:** Square, X Circle, X
- **Bending Reed:** Triangle, Square, X Circle
- **Propeller:** Square, Triangle, X Circle
- **Free Fall:** Triangle, X, X Triangle
- **Burner Speed:** Circle, Circle, Circle, Square
- **Snow Ball:** Triangle, Square, Square, Circle
- **Avalanche:** Triangle, Circle, Circle, Square
- **Rolling Barrel Left:** X Circle, Circle, X
- **Rolling Barrel Right:** X Square, Square, X

STREET FIGHTER EX 3
Successfully complete the original game mode with a regular character without continuing to unlock one of the hidden characters. Another character will be unlocked each time you complete the game. They'll appear in this order:
- Sagat
- Vega
- Garuda
- Shadow Geist
- Kairi
- Pullum
- Area
- Darun
- Vulcano

TEKKEN TAG TOURNAMENT
Accessing modes and beating the game to unlock a secret character are the cheats for TTK.
- If you want to access "Gallery" mode, unlock that devil!
- Wanna get into "Tekken Bowl" mode? Unlock the ogre.

- Beat the game one time to unlock the "Theater" mode.
- How about playing as Doctor Boskonovitch? Then make sure to get the top score in "Tekken Bowl."

SECRET CHARACTERS

Beat the game to unlock each secret character, which are opened in this order:

- Kunimitsu
- Bruce Irvin
- Jack-2
- Lee Chaolan
- Wang Jinrey
- Roger & Alex
- Kuma & Panda
- Kazuya Mishima
- Ogre
- True Ogre
- Prototype Jack
- Mokujin & Tetsujin
- Devil and Angel
- Unknown

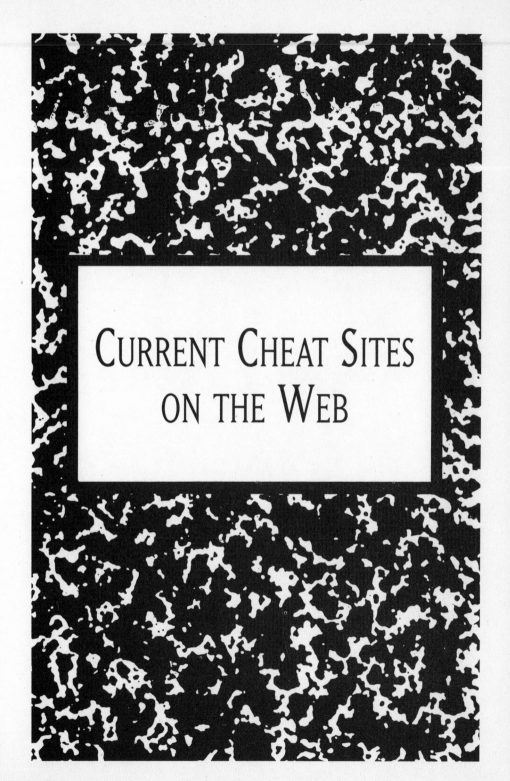

CURRENT CHEAT SITES ON THE WEB

www. cheatcc.com

Cheat Code Central! Its staff calls it "the most comprehensive video and computer game site in the world for Sony PlayStation, PlayStation2, Nintendo 64, Sega Dreamcast, Game Boy, and the PC." Who am I to argue?

www.cheatersguild.com

Features lots and lots of cheats!

www.cheatz.de/index2.shtml

For those of you fluent in German, a cheat site all for you. I can't tell you what it said as I only know French. But it looked cool.

www.gamefan.com/default.asp

Check it out for PS2 stuff as it becomes available. Lots of codes and cheats on this site, plus headlining information about games for PSX, N64, and the PC.

www.gamewinners.com

Reviewed by *Game Start* as containing "just about everything you'll need to beat the games that have been driving you crazy," it features game cheats and help for a large number of games. Check out its PS2 section at www.gamewinners.com/playstation2/index.html

www.thewasteland.co.uk/homepage.htm

The place where the CheatMaster brings you the best tips, cheats, news, and walkthroughs.

www.users.freenetname.co.uk/%7Echeats/sony_systems/playstation_2/playstation_2.htm

This is a new site, and at the time of printing, there wasn't any content, but there should be some soon.

PS2
(AND OTHER GAMING SYSTEMS)
WEB SITES

A Web site is a Web site is a Web site. You can only say so much about the PS2 without repeating other sites, but here are many that offer information ranging from games, features, and cheats for the DVDs and games that are and will play on Sony's next gen box.

www.PlayStation.com
The official Sony site for everything PlayStation.

www.videogames.com
The place to find the Web sites of the *Official U.S. PlayStation Magazine*, *Electronic Gaming Monthly*, and *Expert Gamer*. News, reviews, screenshots, and a whole lot more.

www.psmonline.com
Official Web site for *PSM*, the "100% Independent PlayStation Magazine." Features exclusive columns by the magazine's regular writers, previews of upcoming issues, and desktop images of PlayStation's favorite game girls.

www.gamespot.com
Sister site to videogames.com. Home of *Computer Gaming World*, and the focus at this site is on PC gaming.

www.thefuturenetwork.plc.uk
Home of the British-based *Power–The PlayStation Mag*. News and reviews, tips and cheats.

www.imaginemedia.com

The site that *Next Generation Magazine* calls home, with news and reviews for everything from PS2 to X-Box.

www.psx2.com

Offers PlayStation2 news, features, previews, reviews, and a new addition: dvd.psx2

http://PlayStation.hotgames.com

Gives you cheats, game updates, features, and the Top 20 games.

http://planetps2.com

This site is devoted to everything PS2, no matter what country you live in.

www.ps2k.net

Here's the official countdown site, with more PS2 information.

www.nintendo.com

Check here for all the latest news on N64 and Game Boy, and the most recent developments on Dolphin.

www.sega.com

The place to go for all the in-depth info on the Dreamcast system.

www.gaming-intelligence.com

Diehard fans visit this site for the latest gaming news.

www1.laracroft.co.uk/lara99/front.html

Everything you've ever wanted to know about the pistol-packing heroine of the *Tomb Raider* series, from favorite foods to the latest Eidos spokesmodel.

www.konami.co.jp/kcej/products/west/mgs2/index.html

For all you Solid Snake fans out there, this is the official Konami site for all things related to *Metal Gear Solid*. And don't worry: even though the site's based in Japan, the words are in English.

www.consolenation.com

Hosts many game site domains. Their main site has reviews, editorials, cheats, hardware information.

www.gamingtutor.com/topsites/topsites.html

Provides an index to gaming sites, with descriptions. The list is sorted by the popularity of the site as determined by the number of times the link has been used on Gaming Tutor.

www.the-nextlevel.com

Features PS2, as well as Dreamcast and N64 information. This site offers user forums, plus recent headlines, reviews, previews, and features.

http://guides.ign.com

Features guides (walkthroughs) to many games. The guides are free, but site registration is required.

www.nyko.com/html/main.html

Features add-on hardware for gaming systems, including Sony's. Products include controllers and memory cards, and cables.

www.dailyradar.com/index.shtml

Features breaking Sony news. This site also has an excellent selection of articles.

www.game-revolution.com

"You will find all of life's answers at Game Revolution." Sounds like a Chinese fortune cookie, but you'll find the usual round of reviews, cheats, and game forums here.

http://video.gamespot.co.uk/filters/ps2/home/previews/0,8279,0,00.html

Features a good selection of PS2 games reviews and previews.

www.gamers.com

Features an extensive database of PS2 games and reviews when available. Also included for many games are Web sites for the game, developer, and release dates for future games.

www.vgh.net

Features lots of gaming news with a sarcastic twist.

www.gamesup.com

A content-rich database of game information. Clean site design makes the games easy to find.

www.ga-source.com
A gaming news site.

www.psxgamer.co.uk
Features reviews, previews, and cheats. Not as big of a selection as some sites, but these are Sony only!

www.video-source.com
The folks from this site attend gaming events around the world and present the information on videos you can order through their site. However, if you're not interested in ordering, they also present some of the information for free.

www.rpgamer.com
Features extensive RPG game information.

www.rpg-addicts.com
This is another RPG game site. The site is currently undergoing a redesign.

www.gameguides.com
Features guides (walkthroughs) to many games.

http://gamebase.retrogames.com
A site dedicated to class arcade-style games. Their large database contains lots of information and even some downloads.

http://nebula.spacesports.com/~consoler
The Consolerz site. It bills itself as the place to go for "Next Gen info, latest news, previews, reviews, screenshots."

www.geocities.com/playstation2thefutureishere
Features lots of news and reviews (and some cheats).

POSTSCRIPT

The PS2 game roundup promises to push the gaming envelope. Even with all the amazing new games coming out, it's great to also know that we'll be able to continue playing our classic PlayStation games on this brand new system. Sony has really hit the nail on the head with PS2's combination of features and a price point that isn't out of reach. Anyone who has been considering getting a DVD player will especially appreciate the PS2's DVD playback ability.

Beyond the PS2 graphical and computational muscle also expect broadband technology to be a major force for PS2 gaming. Broadband will integrate with the PS2 through PC Card Ethernet or Firewire, such as DSL and cable modems. The advantages of high speed PS2 connectivity are numerous. Multi-player games are going to be quite popular along with web surfing. We'll likely see some new applications such as video-on-demand and downloadable games.

What does the future hold for the PlayStation? More amazing technology, to be sure, with new levels of kicking graphics and increasing Internet abilities. And the future becomes even more intriguing now that it's become known that Sony has already copyrighted the title "PlayStation3". . . .

Michele E. Davis, PSX guru, spent her youth playing *Centipede* at the Bayport Mall arcade, and dropping transmissions in the parking lot. Finally, she got the amazing Atari 2600 in college—watch out, she can play a mean game of *Frogger*! After the Atari 2600 came the Sega Genesis, and the PSX.

Once the PSX was assembled and in front of the wide-screen TV, Michele spent a marathon session with *Blasto*, no sleep, and lots of Tab®. But it didn't stop with just a big TV. Next came the Svideo cable—a big improvement, and highly recommended for your PlayStation.

Michele's favorite games have been *Silent Hill, Frogger, Centipede*, all the *Tomb Raiders, Crash Bandicoot*, and *Road Rage*.

What is she looking forward to? Amazing graphics in *Nooks and Crannies*, and, having been the only chick in the *Dungeons and Dragons* Club in high school, she is anxiously awaiting *Age of Empires II: The Age of Kings*—and, lastly, plugging her PS2 in to her DSL connection.